The Conscious Mind

Bridging Theology, Science, and Philosophy

by

Dr. ant

The Conscious Mind: Bridging Theology, Science, and Philosophy

Contents

Introduction

Delving into the enigmatic terrain of consciousness, we are confronted with one of the most profound questions that have piqued human curiosity for millennia. What is consciousness? How is it that a collection of neurons and synapses can generate thoughts, feelings, and a sense of self? To grapple with these questions is to engage in a journey that spans theology, science, and philosophy.

The multifaceted nature of consciousness calls for an interdisciplinary approach. Roman Catholics may seek to understand how the immaterial soul aligns with the observable workings of the brain. Skeptics might question the very existence of any non-physical entity influencing our thoughts and behaviors. For psychiatrists, understanding consciousness is imperative not only for treating mental disorders but also for grasping the fundamental nature of human experience. University professors and students across disciplines are similarly drawn to these questions, recognizing that the nature of consciousness is central to debates in metaphysics, ethics, and science.

Our aim is to explore the dimensions and dichotomies that frame the consciousness discourse. We will begin with an expansive look at the nature of consciousness, reviewing definitions and historical perspectives that set the stage for modern inquiry. From René Descartes to contemporary philosophers, the debate continues to evolve, often pivoting around the mind-body problem—an issue so complex it has spawned several competing theories.

The mind-body problem serves as a fulcrum for our exploration. Dualism, which posits the existence of two fundamental substances—mind and body—offers one viewpoint. This doctrine traces its root back to Descartes' famous dictum, "Cogito, ergo sum" ("I think, therefore I am"), yet it faces formidable challenges from an array of alternative theories. Physicalism, for example, asserts that only physical substances exist, thereby requiring a naturalistic explanation for consciousness. Within this framework, debates rage between reductive and non-reductive physicalism, each carrying its own philosophical and empirical complexities.

In the realm of neuroscience, we've witnessed groundbreaking insights into brain structures and functions that presumably underlie conscious experience (Koch, 2004). Case studies and experiments have increasingly underlined the neural correlates of consciousness, emphasizing the brain's intricate architecture. Yet, these insights introduce their own puzzles: How do patterns of neural activity translate into subjective experiences known as 'qualia'?

While physicalist accounts present compelling frameworks, they are not without criticism. To revisit dualism through the lens of contemporary scholarship can be enlightening. Substance dualism, which posits that mind and body are distinct and fundamentally different, contrasts with property dualism, where mental properties emerge from physical substrates but are not reducible to them. Counterarguments to these theories often invoke issues like the causal closure of the physical domain, posing significant hurdles for dualist accounts (Chalmers, 1996).

Our journey doesn't end there. We explore alternative views like panpsychism and emergentism. Panpsychism proposes that consciousness is a fundamental feature of all matter, suggesting a radical rethinking of the physical universe. Emergentism, on the other hand, considers consciousness as an emergent property of complex systems, although what qualifies as 'complex' invites further scrutiny and debate (Strawson, 2006).

Reconciling theological perspectives with scientific findings is an endeavor fraught with both challenges and opportunities. For Roman Catholics and other religious believers, understanding how theology and neuroscience can coexist becomes an exercise in intellectual synthesis. Religious experiences, often deemed subjective and personal, need to be examined for their neural underpinnings without stripping them of their spiritual and existential significance. Can scientific methods and theological insights be mutually illuminating? And if so, how might case studies in religious experiences provide empirical data that contribute to our understanding of consciousness?

Further, we must consider the philosophical implications of various theories. Discussions around free will and determinism often intersect with interpretations of consciousness. If our thoughts and actions are purely determined by neural processes, what becomes of moral responsibility and personal identity? The ethical considerations are profound, affecting everything from legal systems to healthcare practices.

The rapid advancements in science and technology bring new dimensions to the debate. Neuroscientific techniques such as functional magnetic resonance imaging (fMRI) offer unprecedented windows into the brain at work, while innovations in artificial intelligence push the boundaries of what machines can achieve in mimicking human thought processes. These scientific advances necessitate a reassessment of existing theories and open new avenues for research (Dennett, 1991).

Language and communication play pivotal roles in externalizing internal experiences, serving as both a medium and an object of study in consciousness research. Cognitive science perspectives reveal that language is more than a mere descriptor of thoughts; it actively shapes how we think and perceive the world. This has far-reaching implications, especially in the burgeoning field of artificial intelligence, where the quest to develop machines capable of human-like understanding is as much a linguistic feat as it is a technical one.

As we explore the subjective nature of experience, the discussion on 'qualia' and personal experience comes to the forefront. Phenomenology, a philosophical movement spearheaded by thinkers like Edmund Husserl, insists on examining how things appear to consciousness before making any metaphysical commitments about their nature. This approach enriches our understanding of the 'what it is like' aspect of experience, which remains a cornerstone issue in the philosophy of mind.

The problem of other minds also deserves attention. How can we, as conscious beings, ascertain the conscious states of others? This issue has ramifications not only for our interpersonal relationships but also for our interactions with potentially conscious non-human entities, whether animals or advanced AI systems. Here, empirical insights must be complemented by sophisticated theoretical analysis to guide us in drawing responsible and humane boundaries.

Finally, integrative approaches hold promise for advancing our understanding of consciousness. By synthesizing theoretical insights from diverse disciplines and fostering multidisciplinary collaborations, we can hope to build comprehensive models that accommodate the richness and complexity of conscious experience. The future prospects for consciousness research are exciting and teeming with potential, heralding an era where theological, scientific, and philosophical insights coalesce to unravel one of humanity's most enduring mysteries.

In the chapters that follow, we will delve deeper into these themes, dissecting arguments and exploring new perspectives with the rigor and openness that the subject demands. The endeavor to understand consciousness is not just an intellectual exercise; it's a quest to grasp what it means to be truly human.

Chapter 1: The Nature of Consciousness

Consciousness, one of the most enigmatic phenomena known to humanity, has captivated theologians, scientists, and philosophers alike for centuries. It is the ephemeral essence that transcends mere biological substrate to weave the rich tapestry of subjective experience. An attempt to elucidate this awe-inspiring mystery compels us to engage with a multiplicity of perspectives—each offering a distinct lens through which to observe the ineffable. From the dualist assertion of an immaterial mind distinct from the physical body to the starkly contrasting physicalist reduction of consciousness to brain states, the dialogue is as diverse as it is profound (Nagel, 1974). Meanwhile, panpsychism posits that consciousness is a fundamental aspect of all matter, while emergentism argues that consciousness arises from complex physical systems. The convergence of these theories helps us grasp at the fringes of understanding, beckoning us to journey deeper into both the empirical and metaphysical dimensions of this perennial question (Chalmers, 1996; Searle, 2004).

Defining Consciousness

Understanding consciousness involves grappling with questions that span multiple disciplines, from theology and philosophy to neuroscience and psychology. Although a singular, universally accepted definition remains elusive, various frameworks offer valuable insights into what makes the conscious experience unique. At its core, consciousness includes subjective experiences, sense of self, and awareness of both one's external environment and internal states.

At one level, consciousness is often described as the state of being awake and aware of one's surroundings. This operational definition is functional in medical and psychological contexts, distinguishing between various states such as sleep, wakefulness, and altered states induced by substances or medical conditions (Lumer & Rees, 1999). However, this description brushes the surface, failing to encompass the richness and depth of human experience. Scholars often refer to phenomenological properties of consciousness—what it's like to see a color, hear a piece of music, or feel pain. These subjective experiences are a central part of what makes consciousness so intricate and, some argue, inherently mysterious (Nagel, 1974).

In scientific discourse, different approaches seek to elucidate the nature of these experiences. Some researchers focus on identifying the neural correlates of consciousness (NCC)—specific brain states or neural activities that correspond with conscious experiences (Crick & Koch, 1990). Functional magnetic resonance imaging (fMRI) and electroencephalography (EEG) have provided significant insights into what parts of the brain are activated during specific conscious tasks. For instance, the prefrontal cortex is a focal point in understanding higher-order consciousness, related to decision-making and reflective awareness (Baars, 2002). While these studies are indispensable, they also prompt metaphysical queries: Do these neural activities constitute consciousness, or are they merely correlates that accompany another, more fundamental process?

From a philosophical standpoint, defining consciousness also involves grappling with the nature of the mind and its relationship to the body. Cartesian dualism, named after René Descartes, posits that the mind and body are distinct substances, with the mind being non-physical. This dichotomy aims to explain the qualitative aspects of consciousness—the 'what it's like' phenomena—by distinguishing them from purely physical processes (Descartes, 1641). However, dualism faces significant challenges, particularly in explaining how these two substances interact. Critics argue that if the mind is entirely separate from the body, it becomes difficult to understand how mental intentions can cause physical actions (Kim, 2005).

In contrast, physicalist theories propose that mental states are entirely dependent upon or identical to physical states of the brain. Under this banner, reductive physicalists argue that consciousness can be fully explained by understanding physical processes, dismissing the need for non-physical properties or substances (Churchland, 1989). However, this approach often struggles with explaining qualia, the subjective aspects of conscious experience. For instance, the sensory experience of the color red remains an intractable problem for theories that solely rely on physical descriptions. This issue, famously encapsulated by the 'hard problem of consciousness' as articulated by David Chalmers, challenges the notion that physical explanations can ever be fully sufficient (Chalmers, 1996).

While these traditional viewpoints provide foundational perspectives, newer theories like panpsychism and emergentism offer alternative frameworks. Panpsychism suggests that consciousness is a fundamental property of all matter, not something that suddenly appears at a certain level of complexity (Goff, 2017). From this perspective, even single atoms possess rudimentary forms of experience. Though counterintuitive to many, panpsychism bypasses some of the difficulties in explaining the sudden emergence of consciousness in complex organisms.

On the other hand, emergentism posits that consciousness arises from physical processes but cannot be directly reduced to them (O'Connor & Wong, 2015). Like the wetness of water emerging from H2O molecules, consciousness might be an emergent property that cannot be fully understood by examining neurons in isolation. However, this raises additional questions: What laws govern this emergence, and how do they apply uniformly across biological systems?

Adding another layer of complexity, theological perspectives often interpret consciousness as a divine gift, something that transcends physical and even metaphysical explanations. For many adherents, the soul or spirit embodies the conscious self and persists beyond physical existence. This view, particularly present in Roman Catholic thought, intertwines with ethical and moral considerations, influencing beliefs about the sanctity of life and the nature of human dignity (Ratzinger, 1988).

Psychological theories also contribute to the broader discussion by examining how different aspects of consciousness interact. Sigmund Freud's model partitioned the mind into the conscious, preconscious, and unconscious, offering a dynamic perspective on mental life (Freud, 1900). Though Freud's theories have waned in scientific popularity, they remain influential in cultural and therapeutic contexts, emphasizing the layered and often hidden aspects of conscious experience.

Given this rich and multifaceted landscape, it's clear that defining consciousness isn't merely about pinning down a single, definitive explanation. Rather, it involves an interdisciplinary dialogue where scientific, philosophical, and theological perspectives intersect, often challenging and enriching each other. The quest for understanding consciousness is thus not just a technical or academic exercise, but a profound exploration of what it means to be aware, to exist, and to question. This investigation invites us to consider our place in the universe, the essence of our identity, and the very nature of reality itself.

As we move forward in this exploration, each theory and perspective provides unique insights and challenges. The journey doesn't end with a single definition but continues to unfold, revealing layers of understanding that invite us to contemplate the depths of our own existence. It's this complexity—and the ongoing dialogue it inspires—that makes the study of consciousness one of the most formidable yet exciting frontiers in human thought.

Historical Perspectives

The journey into understanding consciousness stretches back thousands of years, featuring the musings of ancient philosophers, the doctrinal declarations of religious figures, and the analytical scrutiny of early scientists. The quest to comprehend the essence of the mind—its faculties, capabilities, and its very nature—traces philosophical thought and religious doctrine through epochs. Contributions from ancient civilizations, medieval scholastics, and early modern thinkers have collectively shaped our contemporary understanding of consciousness.

In ancient Greece, the birth of Western philosophy initiated the foundational discourse on consciousness. Socrates, Plato, and Aristotle set the stage for debate. Socrates' dialogues, often recounted by Plato, raised questions about the soul's immortality and its intrinsic connection to knowledge and reason (Plato, 2007). Plato then expanded these ideas through his Theory of Forms, which posited consciousness as a reflection of eternal, immutable ideas (Ross, 2001). Aristotle, diverging from his teacher, grounded his understanding of the mind in biological processes, suggesting that the soul (psyche) was directly linked to the physical body (Shields, 2016).

Rome saw the inheritance and adaptation of Greek philosophical traditions, with Stoic and Epicurean schools contributing their perspectives. The Stoics embraced a pantheistic worldview, proposing that the soul was part of a cosmic reason (logos) that permeates the universe (Long & Sedley, 1987). Conversely, Epicureans, led by Epicurus and later Lucretius, approached consciousness materialistically, viewing it as an emergent property of the body's atomic arrangements (Fowler, 1998).

The influence of these classical perspectives persisted into the medieval period, where theological thought became the nexus for reflections on consciousness. St. Augustine articulated the Christian synthesis of Platonic ideas with Christian doctrine, focusing on the soul's eternal nature and its journey towards divine truth (Augustine, 1991). Scholasticism, epitomized by St. Thomas Aquinas, brought Aristotelianism into Christian theology. Aquinas advanced an integrated vision where the soul's intellectual and moral capacities were seen as fundamentally interlinked with the embodied human experience (Aquinas, 2006).

During the Renaissance and the dawn of the Enlightenment, the locus of inquiry began to shift from theological constructs to more empirical and rational paradigms. Rene Descartes, a pivotal figure in early modern philosophy, famously declared "Cogito, ergo sum" ("I think, therefore I am"). Descartes posited a strict dichotomy between mind and body, cementing the framework of Cartesian Dualism wherein mental substance (res cogitans) and physical substance (res extensa) interact but remain ontologically distinct (Descartes, 1996).

Subsequent thinkers critiqued and built upon Descartes' dualism. Baruch Spinoza, for instance, rejected Cartesian dualism in favor of substance monism, which held that mind and body were two attributes of a single substance, thus promoting a form of what contemporary philosophers might call panpsychism (Nadler, 2018). Conversely, John Locke and empiricists like David Hume delved into the nature of human understanding and perception, emphasizing the role of sensory experience and contingency in shaping consciousness (Locke, 1975; Hume, 2000).

The advent of the scientific revolution brought about a new era in the study of consciousness, characterized by the integration of rigorous scientific methodologies. Wilhelm Wundt, often considered the father of experimental psychology, established the first laboratory dedicated to psychological research in 1879. Wundt's work underscored the importance of introspection and empirical observation in studying the conscious mind (Wundt, 1902).

The rise of behaviorism in the early 20th century marked a significant divergence from introspection, emphasizing observable behavior over the elusive workings of the mind. Nevertheless, radical behaviorists like B.F. Skinner didn't entirely dismiss consciousness but focused on its study through the lens of behavioral responses to stimuli (Skinner, 1953). Meanwhile, psychoanalysts such as Sigmund Freud explored the unconscious dimensions of the mind, probing into aspects of consciousness that lay beneath the surface of aware experience (Freud, 1964).

In recent decades, advancements in neuroscience have revolutionized our understanding of consciousness. Pioneering research using neuroimaging technologies such as fMRI and PET scans has enabled scientists to investigate the neural correlates of consciousness, bridging the historically vast chasm between philosophical speculation and empirical research (Koch, 2018). These technological innovations provide unprecedented insights, revealing the complex interactions between neural networks and conscious awareness.

This historical excursus reveals that our conception of consciousness has evolved through a myriad of paradigms. From metaphysical inquiries and theological doctrines to scientific exploration and philosophical analysis, each epoch has contributed a unique layer to our comprehension. The ongoing dialogue among theology, philosophy, and science continues to deepen, challenging us to refine and expand our understanding of this profound enigma.

Chapter 2: The Mind-Body Problem

Grasping the essence of the mind-body problem requires navigating an intricate labyrinth where philosophy, theology, and science converge. At the heart of this enigma lies a poignant question: how can immaterial consciousness arise from, or interact with, the physical brain? While some uphold dualism, positing a distinct separation between mind and body, others champion physicalism, asserting that consciousness is merely a product of neural processes (Descartes, 1641; Nagel, 1974). Each theory provides a unique lens through which to examine human experience, from the religious implications of an immaterial soul to the empirical scrutiny of neuroscience. As we dissect these paradigms, we aim to uncover not just the nature of consciousness, but the very essence of human reality.

Dualism

Dualism, a central theme in the mind-body problem, explores the fundamental nature of human existence by positing a clear distinction between the mind and the body. This section seeks to unravel how this centuries-old philosophical concept continues to spark debate among theologians, scientists, and philosophers.

In its basic form, dualism can be traced back to ancient civilizations, but it gained pronounced articulation through the works of René Descartes in the 17th century. Descartes famously argued for the separation of mind and body, coining the phrase "Cogito, ergo sum" or "I think, therefore I am." He proposed that the mind, a non-physical entity, interacts with the body, a physical substrate, through the pineal gland (Descartes, 1641). This dualistic approach assumes that mental states, like beliefs and desires, are not reducible to physical states of the brain, marking a distinct divide between the mental and the corporeal.

From a theological standpoint, dualism aligns closely with many religious traditions that view the soul as distinct from the body. For instance, Christianity often espouses the notion of an immortal soul that survives physical death, thereby supporting a dualistic framework. Saint Thomas Aquinas, integrating Aristotelian principles with Christian theology, argued that while body and soul are distinct, they are also interdependent in humans (Aquinas, 1968). Aquinas' perspective enriched the theological dialogue by emphasizing that although the soul can exist independently, its natural state is to be united with the body.

In contemporary philosophy and science, dualism manifests in various forms, the most prominent being substance dualism and property dualism. Substance dualism maintains that two kinds of substances exist: mental and physical. This view presupposes that mental substances (minds) and physical substances (bodies) exist independently and fundamentally differ in their properties (Robinson, 2020). Minds are characterized by consciousness and intentionality, whereas bodies lack these features and are instead defined by spatial extension and physical properties.

Property dualism, on the other hand, contends that while there is only one kind of substance, it exhibits two distinct sets of properties: physical and mental. This view does not posit a separate mental substance but insists that physical substances, particularly brain states, have both physical properties (such as mass and shape) and mental properties (like beliefs and desires).

A critical challenge to these dualistic views arises from advances in neuroscience, which increasingly elucidate how mental states correlate with brain activity. Functional magnetic resonance imaging (fMRI) and other neuroimaging techniques reveal that specific regions of the brain correspond to distinct cognitive functions. For instance, damage to the Wernicke's area in the brain can impair language comprehension, suggesting a robust linkage between mental capacities and brain structures (Gazzaniga et al., 2018). Such findings pose a significant challenge to substance dualism, urging proponents to clarify how non-physical mental states can causally interact with the physical brain.

Nevertheless, dualism persists, bolstered by arguments concerning subjective experiences or "qualia." Thomas Nagel's seminal essay "What is it like to be a bat?" argues that subjective experiences cannot be fully explained by objective physical processes (Nagel, 1974). This perspective underscores the explanatory gap in physicalist accounts of consciousness and bolsters dualistic theories by emphasizing that subjective experience is fundamentally different from physical description.

Additionally, proponents of dualism argue that physicalism cannot adequately account for intentionality—the 'aboutness' of mental states. Intentionality, the capacity of mental states to be about or represent objects and states of affairs, seems perplexingly absent from purely physical descriptions of brain states. This inadequacy suggests that a dualistic framework might be better suited to explain a range of mental phenomena.

From a theological perspective, dualism continues to resonate with doctrines of the soul's immortality and divine justice. The idea that the soul exists apart from the body supports the belief in an afterlife, a cornerstone in many religious traditions. In Catholic theology, for instance, the soul's immortality is crucial for understanding human destiny and divine judgment (Ratzinger, 1997). This dualistic framework enables a coherent narrative about everlasting life, aligning deeply with faith-based outlooks on human nature and ultimate purpose.

Critics of dualism often point to what is called the "interaction problem," questioning how two fundamentally different substances—mental and physical—can causally interact. This problem was first articulated by Princess Elisabeth of Bohemia in her correspondence with Descartes, highlighting a key difficulty: if mind and body are so different, how can they influence each other? Various solutions have been proposed, including occasionalism and pre-established harmony, but these remain controversial and unconvincing for many.

Despite these critiques, modern variants of dualism, such as the "dual-aspect theory," attempt to reconcile the interaction problem by positing that mind and body are two aspects of the same underlying reality. This proposal suggests a more nuanced understanding that preserves the dualistic insight into the nature of mental states while accepting the scientific evidence for brain-based processes.

In summary, dualism provides a rich and multi-faceted lens through which to examine the mind-body problem. Its historical roots, theological implications, and philosophical arguments offer valuable insights into the nature of consciousness and human existence. While modern science challenges some aspects, dualism remains a potent perspective, capable of evolving and adapting to incorporate new knowledge while addressing age-old questions about mind and matter.

Chapter 3: Ã¢ÂÂ Substances and Properties

In the exploration of consciousness, understanding the fundamental nature of substances and properties serves as a cornerstone for philosophical inquiry. The distinction between substances and properties has been central in metaphysical debates, influencing various theories about the mind and its relationship to the body. To appreciate the nuances of these debates, we must first delve into the essential definitions and frameworks that underpin them.

At its core, a substance is often considered as an entity that exists independently. Aristotle elucidated this concept by identifying substances as those entities that can exist by themselves, such as a tree or a person. Properties, on the other hand, are characteristics or qualities that a substance possesses. These cannot exist independently; for instance, the color green is a property of a leaf, but the color itself cannot float freely without the leaf to embody it (Aristotle, 1995).

The distinction between substances and properties might seem straightforward, yet it opens a Pandora's box of metaphysical puzzles. One classic issue is the problem of universals. If properties are shared, like the greenness of two leaves, how do we account for this shared property while maintaining the individual uniqueness of each leaf? Philosophers have proposed various solutions, ranging from the existence of abstract universals to nominalist views which deny such shared properties altogether.

This tension extends into the mind-body problem, one of the central issues of consciousness studies. Dualists argue for the existence of two distinct substances: the mind and the body. René Descartes famously contended that the mind is a non-material substance with properties such as thought and consciousness, whereas the body is a material substance with physical properties (Descartes, 1996). This form of substance dualism posits that mental properties cannot be reduced to physical properties, underscoring the need for a separate mental substance.

Conversely, physicalists maintain that only one substance exists: the physical. Under this view, what we consider mental properties are either reducible to, or fully explicable by, physical properties of the brain and body. The emergence of neuroscience provides substantial empirical support for physicalist theories, offering explanations for mental phenomena in terms of neural activities and brain structures (Churchland, 1986).

Yet, physicalism faces its challenges. One contentious issue is the problem of qualia—the subjective, individual instances of conscious experience. For example, the experience of the color red is not easily reducible to the physical processes in the brain. Some philosophers argue that qualia exhibit properties which cannot be fully captured by physicalist accounts, hinting at an incompleteness in understanding consciousness purely through physical substances (Nagel, 1974).

Somewhere between strict dualism and physicalism lies property dualism, a nuanced position suggesting that mental properties are non-physical yet do not necessitate a separate mental substance. Property dualists assert that while the brain is a physical substance, it gives rise to both physical and non-physical properties. This view attempts to bridge the gap between acknowledging physical substrates and recognizing the distinctive nature of mental phenomena.

Issues of substances and properties also play a crucial role in emergentist theories. Emergentism posits that higher-level properties arise from the interactions of lower-level substances but are not reducible to those simpler interactions. For instance, consciousness might emerge as a novel property when a system comprising neurons operates in a particular complex manner (Kim, 1999). Here, the emergent properties are neither entirely independent (as in dualism) nor entirely reducible (as in strict physicalism).

The theological implications of these debates cannot be understated. Within Roman Catholic thought, the notion of the soul as a distinct substance aligns closely with dualistic perspectives, though not without modern reinterpretations. The soul, considered the seat of consciousness and moral responsibility, is often argued to have a different essence from the physical body, implicating profound considerations for doctrines of resurrection and immortality (Ratzinger, 2007).

However, integrating these metaphysical distinctions with scientific discoveries urges a multidisciplinary approach. Psychiatrists, for example, must navigate these conceptual waters to better understand mental disorders. From a clinical standpoint, treatments rooted in physicalist frameworks may sometimes prove limiting, urging a broader view that considers potential non-physical properties of the mind.

University professors and students engaged in the study of philosophy, theology, or the nascent field of consciousness studies are thus tasked with threading these complex ideas. The challenge lies in harmonizing empirical findings with robust metaphysical and theological theories, fostering a comprehensive understanding of human consciousness.

The ongoing inquiries into substances and properties thus form a vibrant tapestry of questions and theories. Each perspective, whether dualist, physicalist, or emergentist, brings unique insights while concurrently highlighting the limitations and potentialities of the others. As we march forward in unraveling the intricacies of consciousness, the interplay between substances and properties will remain a critical axis around which much of the debate revolves.

Chapter 4: Ã¢ÂÂ Arguments for Dualism

In examining the mind-body problem, dualism persistently emerges with compelling arguments, often invoking considerations that challenge strict materialist views. Dualism posits that the mental and physical realms are distinct yet interconnected, a notion eloquently suggested by Descartes' cogito argument which underscores the fundamental difference between thinking and extended substances (Descartes, 1641). Contemporary support for dualism also draws from the qualia phenomenon; subjective experiences like pain or the perception of color cannot be reduced merely to neural firings (Chalmers, 1996). Furthermore, the argument from intentionality highlights that mental states about something, such as beliefs or desires, exhibit properties that physical states do not. This dissonance reinforces the dualist assertion that non-physical properties exist (Searle, 1983).

Physicalism

Physicalism, often considered the primary philosophical competitor to dualism, asserts that everything about the mind can be entirely explained in physical terms. At its core, physicalism posits that mental states are nothing more than physical states, governed by the laws of nature without the need for any non-physical substances or properties. This standpoint is appealing to skeptics of metaphysical interpretations, theologians seeking compatibility with scientific perspectives, and those engrossed in the nuances of psychiatric and neurological fields.

The appeal of physicalism comes primarily from its alignment with the empirical methods that underpin contemporary scientific investigation. By rooting mental phenomena in the physical substrate of the brain, physicalism avoids the ambiguities and supernatural implications that frequently plague dualistic theories. One might say it anchors consciousness firmly within the realm of the observable and measurable, removing the necessity for invoking an extrasensory dimension.

In neuroscientific terms, the grounding of mental processes in brain activity has provided a fertile landscape for research. For instance, the identification of neural correlates of consciousness (NCC) has dramatically shifted our understanding of how mental states correspond with brain states. Studies employing functional magnetic resonance imaging (fMRI) and electroencephalography (EEG) have substantially contributed to this understanding, mapping specific patterns of neural activity to particular conscious experiences (Koch et al., 2016).

However, physicalism is not without its philosophical quandaries. A significant critique resides in the explanatory gap problem, famously articulated by Joseph Levine. Levine pointed out that even if we could map every mental state to a brain state, we might still lack an explanation of how exactly these physical processes give rise to subjective experience, a phenomenon often referred to as 'qualia' (Levine, 1983). This gap calls into question whether physicalism can offer a wholly comprehensive account of consciousness.

Moreover, the advent of quantum mechanics, which describes physical reality as fundamentally probabilistic and indeterminate, challenges the strictly deterministic nature of traditional physicalist models. If the brain operates within this quantum framework, could there be aspects of consciousness that elude a purely physicalist interpretation? This question invites further interdisciplinary exploration, drawing from quantum physics, philosophy of mind, and cognitive science.

Ethically, physicalism poses questions about free will and moral responsibility. If all mental states are reducible to physical states governed by causal laws, where does that leave the concept of free will? Some argue that acknowledging consciousness within this framework either diminishes personal agency or compels a redefinition of what free will means in a physicalist paradigm. This is not merely an academic exercise but holds significant implications for jurisprudence, psychiatric evaluation, and ethical theory (Dennett, 2003).

Theologically, physicalism presents challenges and opportunities. It forces a reconciliation between traditional religious views of an immaterial soul and the scientific perspective of a brain-bound consciousness. For Roman Catholics and other religious thinkers, this reconciliation can either be seen as a threat to doctrinal integrity or as an impetus for a deeper understanding of the intersection between faith and reason. Historical anecdotes recount continuous debates within theological circles, reflecting this tension between metaphysical orthodoxy and evolving scientific insights.

Despite these multifaceted challenges, physicalism continues to thrive, not least because of its practicality in medical and psychological disciplines. The success of psychopharmacology, for example, demonstrates physicalism's utility. Medications that affect brain chemistry can elicit profound changes in mood, cognition, and behavior, reinforcing the view that mental states are intimately linked to physical brain states. This pragmatic evidence remains a cornerstone of physicalist argumentation.

It's worth noting that physicalism isn't monolithic. There are flavors, like reductive and non-reductive physicalism, each with its own nuances and implications. Reductive physicalism argues that mental states can be fully reduced to physical states without residue, while non-reductive physicalism suggests that mental states, though grounded in the physical, possess properties that cannot be entirely explained by physical science alone (Stoljar, 2001). Debate continues about these internal distinctions, but all share the conviction that the physical realm is the foundation of all phenomena, including consciousness.

No discussion of physicalism would be complete without addressing the mind-brain identity theory and the principle of supervenience. The identity theory posits that mental states are identical to brain states, much like water is identical to H2O. This view argues against any dualistic separation and supports a seamless integration of mind and body. On the other hand, supervenience suggests a dependent relationship where changes in mental states necessarily follow changes in physical states, even if they are not identically the same. Both ideas strive to explain how consciousness emerges from the material substrate without conceding to dualism's bifurcation.

In sum, physicalism remains a compelling framework for understanding consciousness, supported by a wealth of scientific data and pragmatic applications. It navigates complex philosophical territories, raises essential ethical questions, and challenges theological doctrines, all while adhering to the empirical rigor that modern science demands. As we continue to probe the mysteries of the mind, physicalism will undoubtedly evolve, accommodating new discoveries and addressing unresolved complexities, striving toward a more comprehensive understanding of what it means to be conscious.

Chapter 5: Ã¢Â□Â□ Types of Physicalism

Physicalism, also known as materialism, posits that everything that exists is no more extensive than its physical properties. Essentially, this doctrine proposes that all phenomena, including mental phenomena and consciousness, are a result of physical processes. While this might sound straightforward, there are several varied and complex forms of physicalism. Each offers a different perspective on how traditional metaphysical issues related to the mind and body are to be resolved.

First, let's delve into reductive physicalism. As the name suggests, this form of physicalism asserts that all mental states and properties can be reduced to physical states and properties. For instance, the feeling of pain can be explained utterly by the firing of specific neurons and biochemical processes in the brain. Reductive physicalism leans heavily on the successes of neuroscience and argues that as scientific knowledge expands, it will eventually be able to explain all mental states in purely physical terms (Crick & Koch, 1990).

Another influential form is non-reductive physicalism. This theory grants that while mental states are indeed produced by physical states, they cannot be reduced entirely to physical explanations. In other words, mental and physical states are different aspects of the same reality but retain a certain level of autonomy from each other. Thus, while your joy might arise from neurotransmitter activity, it also has a distinct character that isn't entirely explained by that activity (Kim, 1999).

Then, there's supervenience physicalism, which suggests that any change in mental states necessarily implies a change in physical states. However, it leaves an open question as to the nature of the relationship between these states. What's essential is that mental properties supervene on physical properties, implying that the mental is dependent on the physical in some way. This viewpoint is appealing because it acknowledges a dependency relationship without making strong claims about reducibility (Davidson, 1970).

Functionalism introduces yet another dimension to the understanding of physicalism. It posits that mental states are defined primarily by their functional roles—their causal relations to other mental states, sensory inputs, and behavioral outputs. Put differently, what makes something a 'pain' isn't its physical make-up but rather its role in the system of mental states and processes (Putnam, 1967). This approach is flexible, allowing even for the possibility of artificial intelligence mimicking human consciousness through appropriate functional arrangements.

Eliminative materialism takes a more radical stance by arguing that our common-sense understanding of mental states (known as 'folk psychology') is fundamentally flawed. According to this view, concepts such as beliefs, desires, and feelings don't correspond to any real entities but are rather remnants of an outdated way of thinking. As neuroscience progresses, it will eliminate these notions, replacing them with accurate descriptions of neural states and processes (Churchland, 1981).

Emphasizing the intricacies of each subtype of physicalism helps to appreciate the varied answers the school offers to the mind-body problem. One cannot overlook how different these types of physicalism address the issue of qualia—the subjective experience of mental events. This has been particularly challenging for reductive physicalists because reducing subjective experiences like the taste of chocolate to purely physical terms can be problematic.

Critics of physicalism have often seized upon the theory's difficulties with consciousness and qualia as evidence of its shortcomings. For instance, Frank Jackson's famous 'knowledge argument' challenges reductive physicalism by proposing that there are aspects of knowledge (like knowing what it feels like to see red) that aren't captured by physical explanations (Jackson, 1982). Supervenience and non-reductive physicalists circumvent this critique by positing that while mental states depend on physical states, they encompass more than just the physical.

Finally, it's crucial to address the theological implications of physicalism. This area is a battleground for those reconciling religious views with scientific perspectives. Roman Catholics, for instance, may find non-reductive physicalism more palatable because it allows for the uniqueness of human experience, moral values, and possibly even the soul. On the other hand, reductive physicalism could be troubling due to its potential implications for free will and moral responsibility.

In summation, physicalism offers a diverse array of theories, each providing unique solutions to the enduring mysteries surrounding the mind and consciousness. From reductive physicalism's rigorous neuroscientific grounding to non-reductive physicalism's acknowledgment of the complexities of mental states, the doctrine is far from monolithic. Its ability to address both scientific and philosophical questions makes it a compelling framework, though not without its challenges and criticisms. Understanding these types of physicalism gives us a richer, more nuanced perspective on the ongoing debate about the nature of consciousness.

Chapter 6: Ã¢Â□Â□ Arguments for Physicalism

The discourse surrounding consciousness often swings between competing paradigms, each vying to be the definitive explanation of human experience. In this context, physicalism stands as a potent contender, arguing that all phenomena, including consciousness, are grounded in the physical realm. Physicalism posits that everything that exists is physical or supervenes on the physical, leaving no room for non-material entities. This chapter intends to explore cogent arguments that buttress physicalism, drawing from diverse scientific, theological, and philosophical perspectives.

Arguments for physicalism often begin with the success of the natural sciences in explaining the workings of the world. Physics, chemistry, and biology have progressively demystified phenomena that were once attributed to supernatural causes or metaphysical constructs. For instance, thunder, once thought to be an act of divine anger, is now understood as a natural electrical discharge. This exemplifies a broader trend wherein physical explanations increasingly subsume non-physical ones. The same methodological naturalism underpins the argument that consciousness, too, can be understood in purely physical terms (Dennett, 1991).

Occam's Razor also lends support to physicalism by positing that the simplest explanation, the one that makes the fewest assumptions, is usually the correct one. Physicalism adheres to this principle by positing a single type of substance: the physical. Dualistic theories, in contrast, are more ontologically burdensome, suggesting the existence of both physical and non-physical substances. By obeying the principle of parsimony, physicalism thus provides a more straightforward explanatory framework.

Neuroscientific advancements have further fortified the physicalist position by elucidating the neural correlates of consciousness. Functional magnetic resonance imaging (fMRI) and electroencephalography (EEG) have mapped brain activity correlating with mental states, thereby substantiating the claim that mental phenomena are deeply intertwined with neural processes. Studies investigating the effects of brain lesions have demonstrated that alterations in brain structure can significantly impact cognitive functions, behavior, and personality. This clearly aligns with the physicalist notion that consciousness and mind are rooted in brain activity (Churchland & Churchland, 1983).

In addition, the phenomenon of brain plasticity—which refers to the brain's ability to reorganize itself by forming new neural connections—further underscores the physical basis of mental processes. Through experiences, learning, or following injury, the brain can adapt in ways that affect our mental life. The implication here is that consciousness, cognitive abilities, and even aspects of our personality are largely dependent on the physical structure and functioning of the brain.

However, the robustness of these arguments does not arise in isolation but through a dialogue with historical perspectives. St. Thomas Aquinas, for instance, conceived of the soul as the "form" of the body, fundamentally linked yet somehow distinct. Modern physicalism reinterprets this unity in strictly material terms, claiming that what we call the "soul" could be fully explained by physical processes, a perspective that aims to preserve the integrity of human experience while situating it within a scientific framework.

Physicalists also draw from empirical evidence provided by psychoactive substances, which can alter consciousness in highly predictable ways. These substances interact pharmacologically with brain chemistry to induce changes in perception, cognition, and emotional states. Such observations lend credence to the idea that altering the physical composition of the brain invariably affects the mind, thereby strengthening the physicalist argument.

From a philosophical standpoint, the theory of supervenience supports physicalism. According to this theory, mental states supervene on physical states in such a way that any change in a mental state necessitates a change in the underlying physical state. There is no room for independent mental states; they are entirely dependent on the physical substrate. This is a powerful conceptual tool for arguing that discussing mental phenomena without reference to their physical basis is incomplete, if not entirely misplaced (Kim, 1993).

Moreover, physicalism's explanatory power extends to developmental psychology and evolutionary biology. Developmental psychology demonstrates how cognitive and emotional capacities develop in humans from infancy to adulthood, processes closely linked to brain development. Evolutionary biology, on the other hand, elucidates how cognitive capacities that characterize human consciousness could have evolved through natural selection. Hence, the complex behaviors and cognitive faculties exhibited by humans can be seen as the product of a gradual evolutionary process, entirely grounded in physical mechanisms and evolutionary pressures (Pinker, 1997).

Critically, physicalism also offers compelling arguments for addressing traditional metaphysical issues. Consider the mind-body problem: the question of how mental states like beliefs and desires relate to physical states of the organism. Dualistic solutions often fail to provide a coherent mechanism of interaction between non-physical mental states and physical brain states. In contrast, physicalism, by positing that mental states are brain states, circumvents this problem by denying the need for such interaction entirely. Mental phenomena are simply one aspect of the complex arrangement of physical processes happening in the brain.

Furthermore, the principle of causal closure in the physical domain argues that if physical events can be fully explained by physical causes alone, invoking non-physical causes becomes unnecessary. This directly challenges dualistic paradigms, which posit that non-physical mental states can cause physical events. If every physical event has a sufficient physical cause, as the principle of causal closure states, then non-physical mental events are rendered superfluous—effectively non-entities in a scientifically rigorous description of reality.

It's worth mentioning that physicalism also dovetails well with the operational ethos of contemporary scientific practice, which is rooted in empirical verification and falsifiability. By maintaining a strictly physicalist outlook, scientists ensure that hypotheses remain testable, measurable, and subject to experimental scrutiny. Therefore, physicalism is not just a philosophical stance but one that harmonizes with the methodology and objectives of the empirical sciences.

In summation, physicalism presents itself as a coherent, parsimonious, and empirically robust framework for understanding consciousness. Grounded in the successes of natural sciences, augmented by neuroscientific findings, and philosophically tenable through principles like supervenience and causal closure, it challenges dualistic interpretations of human experience. As our understanding of the brain and its functions deepens, the physicalist paradigm continues to offer compelling explanations, rendering the need for non-material entities increasingly obsolete.

Chapter 7: Neuroscience and Consciousness

The intricate relationship between neuroscience and consciousness invites us into a profound exploration of the brain's architecture and its enigmatic role in generating subjective experiences. By examining brain structures and functions, scientists aim to unravel the neural correlates of consciousness, pursuing the seemingly elusive neural signatures that correspond to conscious states (Koch et al., 2016). This journey is punctuated with enlightening case studies and experiments, such as those involving patients with split-brain syndrome or the utilization of advanced neuroimaging techniques, which reveal fascinating insights about the modular and unified aspects of conscious experience (Gazzaniga, 2005). While empirical data enriches our understanding, the quest to decode consciousness remains interwoven with rich philosophical dilemmas, challenging the boundaries of materialist and dualist perspectives alike. As we delve deeper into the neuroscientific realm, the interplay of biological intricacies and the subjective nature of consciousness offers a fertile ground for both scientific investigation and philosophical contemplation, necessitating a multidisciplinary approach to fully appreciate the depths of human cognition and awareness (Tononi & Koch, 2015).

Brain Structures and Functions

The journey to understanding consciousness inexorably pulls us toward the exquisite and intricate architecture of the human brain. At the core of neuroscience's quest to elucidate the enigmatic nature of consciousness lies a close examination of the brain's various structures and functions. Understanding these components is crucial for bridging the gap between our physical existence and the phenomena of subjective experience.

The cerebral cortex, a wrinkled layer of tissue enveloping the brain, is often associated with the higher functions that many argue are quintessentially human—reasoning, abstract thought, and language. The prefrontal cortex, in particular, stands out as the command center for cognitive control and executive functions. It is this area that facilitates complex behaviors like planning, decision-making, and social interactions—attributes that any theory of consciousness must account for (Miller & Cohen, 2001).

Consider the hippocampus, nestled deep within the temporal lobe. This seahorse-shaped structure is primarily known for its role in memory formation. Its ability to transform short-term memories into long-term ones provides a temporal continuity to our conscious experience. Without this essential function, our sense of self would be fleeting, and we would be perpetually situated in an evanescent "now" devoid of history or future (Squire & Zola-Morgan, 1991).

Then there is the enigmatic amygdala, a small almond-shaped cluster involved in emotional processing. The amygdala's functions complexly intertwine with both the conscious and subconscious realms. It rapidly assesses environmental threats, oftentimes before we are even consciously aware of them. Engaging alarm systems within milliseconds, it influences our fight-or-flight responses. Thus, emotions—an indelible component of conscious experience—are significantly colored by amygdala activity (LeDoux, 1998).

Moving to the thalamus, this central hub acts as the grand relay station for sensory information, channeling data from our senses to various cortical areas. Interestingly, its extensive connectivity makes it a contender for theories positing it as a constituent of the "global workspace," the hypothetical brain-wide web that broadcasts information to numerous specialized modules (Baars, 1988). The thalamus's role in regulating the flow of sensory data could be pivotal in our conscious experience's coherence and unity.

The brainstem, often overlooked in discussions of higher-order processes, is no less critical. It regulates essential functions like heart rate, respiration, and arousal states. Damage to the brainstem can result in states of consciousness such as comas or locked-in syndrome, where one's ability to interact with the external world is immensely compromised. Here, we touch on the delicate balance maintained by the brain between mere survival and thriving in conscious awareness (Britt, Edlow, Wu, & Ullman, 2021).

Let us not forget the basal ganglia—a collection of nuclei dispersed in the brain that finely tunes motor signals and procedural learning. This system becomes particularly salient when we explore phenomena like habituation and skill acquisition, processes that can transition from conscious effort to seemingly automatic actions over time (Graybiel, 2008). The fluidity between conscious and unconscious control exemplifies the complexity and dynamism inherent in brain functions.

Further down the complexity scale, the cerebellum—often considered the "little brain"—plays a substantial role in motor control, balance, and coordination. However, more recent research suggests its involvement in cognitive processes, including attention and language (Schmahmann, 2018). The cerebellum's integration into conscious experience signifies the need to revisit and perhaps revise our compartmentalized views of brain functions.

The corpus callosum, a robust bundle of neural fibers, connects the brain's two hemispheres, ensuring they communicate seamlessly. This interhemispheric dialogue is critical for a unified experience of the world. Consider split-brain patients, whose corpus callosum has been severed to treat epilepsy. These individuals demonstrate that each hemisphere can operate independently, leading to compelling insights into the lateralization and specialization of brain functions (Gazzaniga, 2005).

Diving deeper into the microstructures, the role of neural circuits and networks cannot be overstated. The synaptic connections between neurons form the substrate upon which our thoughts, memories, and emotions build. The concept of neuroplasticity underlines the brain's remarkable ability to reorganize itself by forming new neural connections throughout life in response to learning and experience (Kolb & Gibb, 2011). This adaptability is pivotal in understanding how consciousness can evolve and shift across different states and contexts.

The ascending reticular activating system (ARAS), originating in the brainstem, also deserves mention. It plays a crucial role in regulating wakefulness and sleep-wake transitions by projecting to various brain regions, thereby modulating cortical activity. The ARAS ensures that our brain remains attuned to the external environment during wakefulness while transitioning to different states during sleep, including dreams which are forms of consciousness on their own (Moruzzi & Magoun, 1949).

In the realm of cognition and human experience, electrical and chemical signals traverse these brain structures, mediating various states of awareness. One could argue that understanding the functionality of neurotransmitters—chemical messengers like dopamine, serotonin, and acetylcholine—is equally significant. These chemicals regulate mood, attention, and arousal, directly influencing our conscious states (Nutt et al., 2007).

The brain structures and functions thus form a symphony of components working in concert. Each structure, while having specialized roles, is remarkably interconnected, embodying a system where the whole is indeed greater than the sum of its parts. They provide the scaffolding upon which consciousness manifests—a point of intersection for theologians, philosophers, and scientists alike. The nature of this intersection invites us to explore not just how consciousness arises from these structures, but why it does so in the manner it does.

A nuanced understanding of brain structures and their functions offers crucial insights into the essential nature of consciousness. It encourages us to reflect on the profound connection between our physiological makeup and our subjective experiences. Philosophical questions mesh seamlessly with empirical investigations, forging a path that examines consciousness's multifaceted nature. As we proceed to further sections, let us appreciate the complexity and subtlety required to unravel the mysteries of the conscious mind.

Neural Correlates of Consciousness

The quest to comprehend consciousness has been an enduring one, traversing through various domains of philosophy, theology, and, in contemporary times, neuroscience. The concept of neural correlates of consciousness (NCC) serves as a crucial bridge in this quest, connecting the immaterial aspect of conscious experience with the physical reality of neural activity. As we delve into this section, the goal is to elucidate how neuroscience endeavors to pinpoint specific brain structures and functions that correlate with the multitudinous aspects of conscious experience.

Firstly, it's important to discuss what we mean by NCC. At the most basic level, neural correlates of consciousness refer to the minimal set of neural events and structures sufficient for a particular conscious percept or experience. The precise identification of these structures and events is key to understanding how subjective experiences arise from physical processes. An array of techniques, from neuroimaging to electrophysiology, has been deployed to map these links. Yet, the quest to isolate the NCC raises fundamental questions about the nature of consciousness itself.

Let's consider the role of the cerebral cortex. Many studies point to the significance of cortical regions, notably the prefrontal and parietal cortices, in orchestrating conscious experience (Koch et al., 2016). Functional Magnetic Resonance Imaging (fMRI) and Electroencephalography (EEG) have shown that activation in the prefrontal cortex often correlates with high-level cognitive functions, including decision-making, attention, and intentionality. When we ponder a moral dilemma or solve a complex problem, it is likely these regions that are actively engaged. Conversely, damage to these areas often results in specific deficits in conscious awareness, providing a direct hint of their importance.

However, the story doesn't end with the cortex. The midbrain structures, such as the thalamus, play an equally pivotal role. The thalamus acts as a relay station, facilitating communication between different cortical areas and modulating the flow of sensory information. Intriguingly, studies using deep brain stimulation have shown that stimulating certain areas of the thalamus can restore consciousness in individuals in a vegetative state, underscoring its integrative function (Schiff, 2010).

Furthermore, it is crucial to tackle the conundrum of how these neural activities translate into the rich tapestry of subjective experience. This is where the philosophical debates intertwine with empirical findings. Dualists might argue that no matter how detailed our neural maps become, they will never fully capture the qualia—the individual instances of subjective, conscious experience. Meanwhile, physicalists maintain that a complete understanding of NCC will eventually illuminate the nature of consciousness.

An intriguing perspective within physicalism is the "Global Workspace Theory" proposed by Bernard Baars. This theory posits that consciousness is a product of information being broadcast to various specialized processors in the brain, much like a global workspace or a shared blackboard. Neuroimaging studies have lent support to this model by showing that conscious perception is often accompanied by widespread cortical activation (Dehaene & Changeux, 2011). The widespread nature of these neural signals suggests that consciousness might involve large-scale brain integration rather than a localized phenomenon. This insight aligns well with the theological view that sees human consciousness as integrated and holistic, reflecting a complex unity that is more than just the sum of its parts.

Another promising model is the "Integrated Information Theory" (IIT) championed by Giulio Tononi. IIT seeks to quantify the level of consciousness by the degree of integrated information within a system. According to this model, the thalamocortical system, due to its high level of complexity and integration, is posited to be the primary substrate for consciousness (Tononi, 2008). IIT has pushed the frontier by moving beyond mere correlation to propose a metric for consciousness, offering a novel approach to understanding NCC, even if it still faces empirical and philosophical challenges.

While theories are abound, empirical research provides another avenue through case studies and experiments. One telling observation is the phenomenon of "blindsight" where individuals with damage to their primary visual cortex can respond to visual stimuli they do not consciously perceive (Weiskrantz, 1997). Blindsight reveals that consciousness isn't merely a byproduct of sensory processing but rather requires a more intricate network of neural interactions. Here, the distinction between mere neural activity and the conscious experience becomes starkly evident.

Moreover, modern advancements in neurotechnology, like Brain-Computer Interfaces (BCIs) and optogenetics, have opened new vistas for probing the NCC. BCIs, by translating neural signals directly into action, offer a tangible modality to understand how specific patterns of neural activity correlate with specific conscious intentions. Optogenetics allows for the control of neural activity with light, enabling researchers to manipulate neural circuits with unprecedented precision.

Yet, for all its advancements, neuroscience faces the "hard problem" of consciousness, a term coined by philosopher David Chalmers. The hard problem refers to the question of why certain physical states are accompanied by conscious experience. While we might determine how neural mechanisms work, explaining why they give rise to conscious experience remains an elusive challenge. This reflects a fundamental theological and philosophical query about the nature of existence and the divine spark within human beings.

Theologically, one might view the NCC as the means through which a higher power manifests conscious experience in the material world. This perspective does not diminish the empirical endeavor but rather enriches it, proposing that neural correlates are the instruments of a grander design. Consciousness, from this vantage, becomes the interface between divine intentionality and human experience.

In summary, the neural correlates of consciousness represent a fascinating and complex interplay between brain structures, neural activities, and subjective experiences. The advances in neuroscience—from identifying critical brain regions like the cortex and thalamus to developing integrative theories and cutting-edge technologies—bring us closer to unraveling this mystery. However, this endeavor continually intersects with deep philosophical and theological questions, making the study of NCC not just a scientific quest but also a profound journey into the essence of what it means to be conscious.

The pursuit of understanding NCC is ongoing, and it invites a multidisciplinary approach, requiring the insights from philosophy, theology, and advanced scientific research. As we progress, we are reminded of the words of the Apostle Paul: "For now we see through a glass, darkly; but then face to face" (1 Corinthians 13:12). The neural correlates of consciousness may yet hold the key to lifting that veil, even if slightly.

Case Studies and Experiments

In the quest to better understand consciousness through the lens of neuroscience, numerous case studies and experiments have yielded pivotal insights. These investigations often serve as a bridge between lofty philosophical theories and empirical data, enriching our comprehension of the mind-body problem.

One extensively studied case is that of Phineas Gage. In 1848, Gage survived a grievous accident in which an iron rod pierced through his skull, damaging parts of his frontal lobe. Remarkably, he lived but exhibited drastic changes in personality and behavior. This led to significant advances in our knowledge about the role of the frontal lobes in personality, cognition, and decision-making processes. Gage's case laid the groundwork for modern neuropsychology by emphasizing the intricate relationship between brain structures and functions, underlining the idea that consciousness and personality are deeply intertwined with neural substrates (Macmillan, 2000).

Another profound case is that of Henry Molaison, often referred to as H.M., whose hippocampus was surgically removed to treat severe epilepsy. The surgery alleviated his seizures but also resulted in anterograde amnesia, the inability to form new memories. This unintentional outcome signified that the hippocampus plays a crucial role in memory formation. H.M.'s condition provided empirical support for the theory of localized brain functions, suggesting that certain cognitive faculties are confined to specific brain regions (Scoville & Milner, 1957).

Experiments involving split-brain patients, who have had the corpus callosum severed to treat epilepsy, also provide valuable insights. These studies reveal that each hemisphere of the brain can function independently and even exhibit distinct personalities and preferences. For example, a split-brain patient might be able to name objects held in the right hand (processed by the left hemisphere, where the speech centers are located) but fail to do so with objects in the left hand (Gazzaniga et al., 1962). These findings further our understanding of the lateralization of brain functions and suggest that consciousness might not be a singular, unified entity but a collection of processes possibly distributed across different cerebral regions.

Neuroscientific experiments also delve into the neural correlates of consciousness (NCC). These studies aim to identify specific brain activities linked to conscious experiences. Christof Koch and Francis Crick proposed that specific patterns of neural activity, possibly in synchrony within the 40 Hz range, could be responsible for the unified nature of consciousness (Koch, 2004). Experiments utilizing functional magnetic resonance imaging (fMRI) and electroencephalography (EEG) have investigated sensory awareness, attention, and self-awareness, identifying regions like the prefrontal cortex and posterior parietal cortex as integral to conscious experience (Dehaene & Changeux, 2011).

Experimentation with psychedelics has opened another realm of investigation. Psilocybin, the active compound in "magic mushrooms," has been shown to increase the connectivity between different brain regions, altering consciousness in profound ways. Studies have also shown that psilocybin induces a temporary reduction in the activity of the default mode network (DMN), a collection of brain regions associated with self-referential thought processes. These findings suggest that altering the DMN's activity can lead to mystical or transcendent experiences, expanding the scope of what consciousness can entail (Carhart-Harris et al., 2012).

Studies on patients with disorders of consciousness, such as vegetative states, also contribute significantly to our knowledge. With the advent of advanced imaging techniques like fMRI and positron emission tomography (PET), scientists can detect residual brain activity in patients who outwardly show no signs of awareness. In a groundbreaking study, Adrian Owen and his team discovered that some patients seemingly in a vegetative state could respond to yes-or-no questions by modulating their brain activity in specific ways detectable by fMRI (Owen et al., 2006). These findings challenge the boundaries of medical definitions of consciousness and prompt ethical debates on the treatment and care of such patients.

The controversial and enigmatic field of near-death experiences (NDEs) also merits attention. Research by Pim van Lommel and colleagues examined cardiac arrest survivors who reported vivid, coherent experiences during periods of clinically recorded brain inactivity. These accounts often include perceptions of moving through a tunnel, seeing a bright light, and feelings of peace or detachment from the body. The phenomenon remains largely unexplained but suggests that consciousness might transcend traditional neural explanations (van Lommel et al., 2001).

In another intriguing domain, experiments involving brain-computer interfaces (BCIs) illustrate the convergence of technology and consciousness. BCIs enable direct communication between the brain and external devices, allowing individuals to control computers or prosthetic limbs through thought alone. These advancements not only aid those with severe disabilities but also offer insights into the neural mechanisms underlying intentionality and volition. Such studies highlight the brain's extraordinary plasticity and capability for adapting to new modes of interaction, furthering our understanding of the neural basis of will and action (Thompson, 2019).

Lastly, the use of transcranial magnetic stimulation (TMS) and direct current stimulation (tDCS) has provided novel ways to explore the malleability of consciousness. By applying these methods, researchers can temporarily disrupt or enhance neural activity in targeted areas of the brain. Experiments have shown that stimulation of the prefrontal cortex can result in enhanced cognitive functions, such as improved problem-solving skills and working memory. Conversely, disrupting activity in this area can impair these functions, thereby mapping out regions integral to conscious thought and cognitive operations (Fregni et al., 2005).

Collectively, these case studies and experiments form the empirical backbone of our understanding of consciousness in its myriad forms. They provide tangible data that can be juxtaposed against philosophical and theological hypotheses, contributing to the rich tapestry of the mind-body discourse. By balancing empirical observations with theoretical explorations, we move closer to untangling the complex enigma that is human consciousness.

As we traverse through these varied studies, one thing becomes clear: Consciousness is not a monolithic phenomenon but comprises many facets, each interwoven with the functions and structures of the brain. These intricate connections between neural activities and conscious experiences beckon further investigation, inviting a multidisciplinary approach that encompasses neuroscience, philosophy, theology, and beyond.

Chapter 8: Dualism Revisited

As we return to the concept of dualism, it is imperative to dissect its intricacies through both substance and property dualism, dissecting their inherent differences and implications. Substance dualism posits that mind and body are entirely distinct entities, raising foundational questions about the nature of interaction between two disparate substances (Descartes, 1641). Meanwhile, property dualism suggests that mental properties are non-physical attributes emerging from physical substances, but without their own independent existence (Kim, 2005). The revival of dualism in contemporary discourse is not without its criticisms; some argue that it fails to account for advancements in neuroscience that increasingly suggest a more monistic understanding of consciousness (Churchland, 1986). Nonetheless, the intuitive appeal of dualism persists, primarily because it resonates with our subjective experiences and keeps open the dialogue between science and metaphysical inquiry. Though it faces considerable opposition, dualism's nuanced perspectives continue to challenge our understanding of the mind-body relationship.

Substance Dualism

In our exploration of dualism, substance dualism stands out as one of the most significant and debated theories. Rooted in Cartesian philosophy, it posits that the mind and body are two distinct substances that interact but are fundamentally different in their essences. Rene Descartes, one of the key proponents of this theory, argued that the mind, or "res cogitans," is a non-material, thinking entity, while the body, or "res extensa," is a material, extended entity (Descartes, 1641/1985).

The allure of substance dualism lies in its intuitive appeal. For many, there is a palpable feeling that "mental" experiences—thoughts, emotions, desires—are categorically different from physical processes such as biological functions and neural firings. This distinction was reiterated by modern philosophers like E.J. Lowe, who argued that psychological states have a first-person ontology, whereas physical states have a third-person ontology (Lowe, 1996).

However, this view is not without its critics. The "interaction problem," first discussed by Princess Elisabeth of Bohemia in her correspondence with Descartes, challenges the coherence of substance dualism. If the mind and body are entirely distinct, how do they interact? Descartes proposed that this interaction occurs in the pineal gland, but modern science has not substantiated this claim.

In attempting to grapple with the interaction problem, some dualists have resorted to more elaborate metaphysical frameworks. For instance, Karl Popper and John Eccles introduced the concept of the "dualist interactionism," proposing that the mind can influence the probability of neuron firing patterns without violating the laws of physics (Popper & Eccles, 1977). While intriguing, such theories often face methodological challenges in empirical validation.

Furthermore, advances in neuroscience have added layers of complexity to the mind-body debate. Neuroimaging studies reveal that mental activities, such as decision-making and emotional responses, correlate with specific neural activities (Gazzaniga, 2000). While substance dualists could argue this correlation does not imply causation—a classic post hoc ergo propter hoc fallacy—physicalists counter that such evidence strengthens the case for a monistic perspective on consciousness.

Still, substance dualism maintains a resilient presence in both academic and popular thought, partly due to its alignment with certain theological doctrines. Many religious traditions, particularly within Christianity, endorse a dualistic view of human nature, where the soul is distinct from the body. This perspective aligns with the doctrine of the immortality of the soul—a foundational belief in Roman Catholic theology (Ratzinger, 2006).

Notably, Thomas Aquinas, though often categorized as a hylomorphic dualist, offered a nuanced perspective. He posited that while the soul and body are different, they form a composite unity. This Thomistic framework can be seen as a bridge between strict substance dualism and more integrative approaches (Aquinas, ST I, Q. 75, Art. 2).

Critics also argue that substance dualism does not adequately address the phenomenological continuity of experience. Husserlian phenomenology and phenomenological psychiatry emphasize the lived experience, which does not neatly divide into "mental" and "physical" realms. According to this view, consciousness and embodiment are intertwined in a seamless fabric of experience (Merleau-Ponty, 1962).

Given these critical perspectives, substance dualism must continuously refine its arguments. For example, modern proponents often draw on quantum mechanics to suggest that consciousness might operate in dimensions beyond the classical physical framework (Stapp, 2007). These speculative theories, while intriguing, remain on the fringes of mainstream scientific acceptance.

One must also consider the philosophical implications of substance dualism, especially concerning personal identity and free will. If the mind is a distinct substance, it allows for the possibility of an enduring self that transcends physical death. This has profound implications for discussions on the afterlife, reincarnation, and the nature of personal identity.

Conversely, physicalist theories must account for identity through continuity of physical processes and memories.

In psychiatric practice, the mind-body dichotomy presents unique challenges. Traditional psychiatric models often compartmentalize mental disorders into either "psychological" or "biological" causes. Substance dualism suggests a more inclusive approach, where therapeutic interventions might need to address both mental and physical dimensions (Kendler, 2005).

Ultimately, substance dualism remains a vital component of the broader conversation about consciousness. While it faces significant challenges from both scientific and philosophical circles, its enduring appeal and the depth of questions it raises ensure its continued relevance. As we revisit dualism, substance dualism provides a fertile ground for debate, encouraging deeper inquiries into the nature of human existence and the enigmatic relationship between mind and body.

Property Dualism

In revisiting dualism, the notion of property dualism emerges as a critical conceptual framework. Unlike substance dualism, which posits that mind and body are composed of fundamentally different substances, property dualism suggests that there is only one kind of substance—usually physical—but this substance possesses two distinct types of properties: physical and mental. This perspective provides a bridge between the stark dichotomy traditionally seen in substance dualism and offers a nuanced view that aligns more closely with contemporary scientific understandings of the brain and consciousness.

To delve deeper, property dualism posits that mental properties, such as beliefs or sensations, are non-physical attributes that cannot be fully explained by physical properties alone. For example, while the brain can be described in terms of neurons, synapses, and biochemical processes, the subjective experience of pain or the color red—often referred to as qualia—exhibits features that seem resistant to a purely physical description. This idea is supported by the notable 'knowledge argument' proposed by philosopher Frank Jackson. Jackson's thought experiment involving "Mary the color scientist" illustrates that complete physical knowledge of a phenomenon does not necessarily entail knowledge of its qualitative aspects (Jackson, 1982).

The implications of property dualism are far-reaching, particularly in the fields of psychiatry and neuroscience. Psychiatric conditions often blur the lines between physical and mental properties, challenging practitioners to adopt a holistic approach. For instance, major depressive disorder can be understood in terms of chemical imbalances and neural circuitry but also requires an appreciation of patients' subjective experiences and emotional states to be effectively treated. This dual approach aligns with the property dualist perspective that mental properties are irreducible to purely physical explanations.

Though property dualism offers an appealing middle ground, it is not without its criticisms. One significant challenge is explaining how non-physical mental properties can causally interact with the physical brain, a point often raised by critics who argue for a more parsimonious physicalist viewpoint (Kim, 2005). Proponents respond by suggesting that mental properties arise from, yet are not reducible to, physical properties —a concept akin to emergent properties in systems theory. Just as the wetness of water cannot be reduced to the properties of individual H_2O molecules, mental properties could be seen as emergent features of complex neural systems.

From a theological perspective, property dualism can be harmonious with certain religious doctrines. The Roman Catholic Church, for instance, has long maintained that the soul is a real entity distinct from the body, but also acknowledges the integrated nature of human beings. The concept of property dualism allows for a structured interpretation where the soul's influence might be seen through the unique mental properties arising from physical human bodies. As Pope John Paul II articulated, the relationship between the body and the soul is not one of mere juxtaposition but an intimate union (John Paul II, 1998).

Philosophically, property dualism finds itself at an intersection, borrowing elements from both dualistic and physicalist traditions. It demands a rigorous inquiry into the nature of properties themselves. Are mental properties fundamental, or can they be explained away by future scientific advancements? Given our current limitations in understanding consciousness, property dualism serves as a provisional yet robust framework that challenges both extreme dualistic and reductive physicalist accounts.

In the educational sphere, property dualism provides a fertile ground for academic exploration, particularly for students and professors in philosophy departments. It invites a reconsideration of classical texts and encourages engagement with cutting-edge scientific research, fostering an interdisciplinary approach. This is not merely theoretical; real-world applications in AI, cognitive science, and neuroethics hinge on our understanding of the mind-body relationship.

Furthermore, property dualism can recalibrate ethical considerations in medical practice and research. If mental properties have an irreducible nature, this elevates the moral status accorded to individual experiences. Patient autonomy and informed consent, for instance, hinge upon recognizing the full scope of a person's mental (and therefore moral) landscape. In this way, property dualism isn't just a metaphysical stance but a perspective with tangible ethical ramifications.

Finally, scholars must consider the evolution of the debate. Historical perspectives have provided foundational insights, but advancing technology and methodological breakthroughs in neuroscience continually reshape our understanding. Future empirical research, particularly in exploring the neural correlates of consciousness, may either bolster or challenge the tenets of property dualism. It remains an open question, ripe for scholarly investigation, whether future discoveries will support this framework or necessitate the emergence of a new paradigm.

Indeed, the rich dialogue between theology, science, and philosophy hints at an even more layered understanding of consciousness that goes beyond current frameworks. As we ponder the intricate tapestry of mental and physical properties, property dualism invites us to navigate this complexity with both an open mind and a critical eye.

Criticisms and Counterarguments

Revisiting dualism inevitably invites a slew of criticisms and counterarguments that persist despite its enduring allure. One of the primary criticisms leveled against dualism is its apparent failure to provide a coherent interaction between the mind and body. René Descartes posited that the pineal gland might be the site where the immaterial mind influences the physical body (Descartes, 1641). However, this notion has been largely dismissed by the scientific community as anatomically unfounded. How can an immaterial entity, which lacks physical properties, produce an effect in the physical realm? The crux of this criticism lies in the elusive "interaction problem," where dualists struggle to explain the mechanism by which the immaterial mind and material body influence each other.

Moreover, the advancements in neuroscience present formidable challenges to dualism. Empirical findings have shown that mental states often correlate directly with brain activity. Functional magnetic resonance imaging (fMRI) scans reveal that specific thoughts and feelings correspond with distinct neural patterns and structures (Linden, 2006). If mental states can be traced to neurophysiological processes, dualists must account for this apparent redundancy. The so-called "neural correlates of consciousness" provide a detailed map that suggests consciousness is a product of physical processes, reinforcing the physicalist view.

Philosophers such as Gilbert Ryle have also criticized dualism for what he termed the "category mistake" (Ryle, 1949). According to Ryle, dualists erroneously treat the mind as an entity akin to a physical object. This perspective, he argues, arises from linguistic confusions. The mind should not be considered a "thing" but rather a set of capacities and behaviors. This behaviorist critique challenges the fundamental assumptions of dualism by deconstructing the very language used to describe mental phenomena.

Another potent criticism comes from the principle of parsimony, often referred to as Occam's Razor. This principle posits that among competing hypotheses, the one with the fewest assumptions should be selected. Dualism posits the existence of two distinct substances—mind and body—unnecessarily complicating our ontology. Physicalists argue that their framework, which invokes only physical substances, is simpler and therefore more parsimonious. Indeed, the principle of parsimony stands as a significant theoretical advantage for physicalism over dualism.

Critics also point to evolutionary biology as undermining the dualistic framework. From an evolutionary standpoint, consciousness and mental states must have arisen through natural selection and therefore have a material basis. Proponents of physicalism argue that evolutionary processes offer a plausible and empirical explanation for the emergence of consciousness, dismissing the need for a non-material mind. Dualism, from this view, appears incompatible with the continuity implied in evolutionary theory (Dennett, 1991).

Philosopher David Chalmers introduces yet another complex nuance in the discussion through his concept of "hard problems" of consciousness (Chalmers, 1996). According to Chalmers, while physical processes can explain the "easy problems" (such as perception, learning, and memory), they fall short in addressing why these processes are accompanied by subjective experience. Surprisingly, Chalmers' arguments are sometimes employed both in support of and against dualism. Critics assert that his acknowledgment of the "hard problem" does not necessitate dualism but invites more sophisticated physicalist or emergentist models.

While dualists argue that subjective experiences (qualia) point toward a non-material aspect of consciousness, critics counter that invoking non-material explanations is an argument from ignorance. They argue that just because science has yet to fully explain consciousness does not necessitate a leap to dualism. Instead, it calls for a more detailed and nuanced scientific investigation into the properties of physical systems.

Additionally, dualism faces epistemic challenges. If the mind and body are separate, how can we have any knowledge of other minds? This is often referred to as the "problem of other minds." If mental states are not directly observable and are not physical, how can one entity infer the existence of another's mental state? Critics argue that this leads to a form of solipsism, where one's own mind might be the only verifiable existence, a position that is philosophically and practically untenable.

The idea of substance dualism has also been met with resistance from proponents of modal logic. Saul Kripke, for instance, has argued that while we can conceive of the mind existing without the body, this does not necessitate their actual separation. Conceptual possibility does not entail metaphysical reality (Kripke, 1980). This modal critique undermines the argument that conceivable distinctions between mind and body substantiate metaphysical dualism.

Despite these criticisms, dualism does have its defenders who present counterarguments aiming to bolster its credibility. Some philosophers invoke the notion of non-reductive dualism, suggesting that mental and physical states are distinct but not wholly independent entities. This position attempts to reconcile the interaction problem by positing a complex, layered reality where mind and body interact seamlessly, though not reducibly to one another.

The theological perspective often lends support to dualist views, arguing that human beings possess souls that cannot be entirely explained through physical means. Religious traditions such as Roman Catholicism traditionally support doctrines of the soul's immortality, which aligns closely with dualistic interpretations of human nature (Catechism of the Catholic Church, 1993). However, even within religious circles, debates persist about how to reconcile such views with contemporary scientific understandings.

In light of these multi-faceted criticisms and counterarguments, it becomes clear that the debate surrounding dualism is far from settled. The enduring questions about the nature of consciousness, the explanatory power of neuroscience, and the philosophical implications of mind-body interactions ensure that dualism remains a significant, albeit contested, theory in the exploration of consciousness.

Chapter 9: Physicalist Theories

Physicalist theories, by positing that all mental states and consciousness itself are ultimately physical in nature, emerge in stark contrast to dualistic perspectives. Reductive physicalism asserts that mental phenomena can be fully explained through physiological and neurological processes, reducing consciousness to purely physical terms without remainder (Stoljar, 2015). On the other hand, non-reductive physicalism allows for mental states to be seen as properties of physical systems that can't be fully reduced to or explained by lower-level physical laws alone, suggesting an emergent complexity akin to other scientific phenomena (Bickle, 2021). Yet, these theories face significant challenges, both empirically and philosophically, particularly in addressing how subjective experience and qualia arise from objective neural processes (Chalmers, 1996). The ongoing debates highlight the complexity and revolutionary implications of understanding consciousness within a physicalist framework, continually bridging gaps between neuroscience, philosophy, and theology without diminishing the rich, subjective tapestry of human experience.

Reductive Physicalism

Reductive physicalism stands as one of the pivotal theories within the broader umbrella of physicalist thought. At its core, reductive physicalism posits that all mental states and properties can be reduced to and explained by physical states and properties. The essence of this perspective asserts that consciousness and all its complex phenomena are ultimately grounded in the physical workings of the brain and nervous system. From this standpoint, mental realities do not exist independently but are rather manifestations of physical processes. Therefore, understanding the physical intricacies of the brain can lead to a comprehensive understanding of consciousness.

Historically, the roots of reductive physicalism can be traced back to classical materialism, where philosophers like Democritus proposed that everything in the world, including mind and soul, could be broken down into material components. In the 20th century, these ideas evolved alongside advancements in science and technology, giving rise to more sophisticated forms. Particularly in the realm of neuroscience, researchers began uncovering direct correlations between specific neural activities and mental experiences, bolstering the claims of reductive physicalists.

One of the main arguments supporting reductive physicalism is the principle of causal closure in the physical domain, which states that if physical events can be fully explained by physical causes, then introducing non-physical causes becomes superfluous. The brain, as a physical entity, orchestrates behavior, and no additional "mental substance" is required. For example, if every emotion, thought, and decision can be mapped onto neural circuits and biochemical processes, then invoking a separate mental realm loses its explanatory necessity. This is not just an assertion but a cornerstone of many scientific methodologies, particularly within cognitive neuroscience (Bickle, 2019).

Studies in brain imaging technologies, such as fMRI and PET scans, have provided empirical support to reductive physicalism by vividly illustrating how specific brain areas activate in correlation with particular mental states. For instance, the activation of the amygdala is often linked to emotional reactions, while prefrontal cortex activity is associated with decision-making and reasoning. These findings demonstrate that what we experience as thoughts, feelings, or even spiritual insights can be traced back to tangible, physical events in the brain (Gazzaniga, 2005).

Philosopher Jaegwon Kim put forward influential arguments in favor of reductive physicalism, particularly through his work on the causal exclusion problem, which challenges the notion that mental events can have causal powers independent of physical events. Kim's argument rests on the presumption that if physical events can explain mental events without residue, then postulating any extra causal power for mental events is redundant and unnecessary (Kim, 2005). Thus, the explanatory power of physicalism lies in its capacity to provide a unified framework where physical processes comprehensively account for mental phenomena.

Despite its compelling framework, reductive physicalism faces several criticisms. One notable challenge is the "hard problem" of consciousness, articulated by philosopher David Chalmers. This problem critiques the ability of reductive physicalism to account for subjective experiences or qualia— the rich, first-person experiences that are intrinsic to being a conscious agent. While reductive physicalism excels at addressing the "easy problems" of consciousness, such as explaining cognitive functions and behavioral outputs, it struggles to explain why and how subjective experience arises from physical processes (Chalmers, 1996).

Reductive physicalists often counter this criticism by arguing that what seems incomprehensible today may not remain so indefinitely. They assert that as neuroscience and related fields advance, more comprehensive explanations for qualia could emerge. Just as complex phenomena like life and heredity have found physical explanations through centuries of scientific progress, so too might consciousness eventually be understood in strictly physical terms.

Another significant critique involves the notion of multiple realizability, proposed by Hilary Putnam. According to this idea, mental states can be realized in multiple ways across different substrates. If mental states can exist in beings with fundamentally different physical compositions (e.g., silicon-based life forms), it implies that mental properties are not necessarily reducible to any particular physical substrate. This poses a problem for reductive physicalism, which relies heavily on a one-to-one mapping between mental states and physical states (Putnam, 1975).

Nevertheless, proponents of reductive physicalism often dismiss the multiple realizability objection by suggesting that it does not sufficiently undermine the central thesis, that mental states are firmly rooted in physical states. Even if different substrates can host similar mental states, the fashion in which these mental states are instantiated remains a physical process. Thus, reductive physicalism retains its viability by focusing on the principle that all mental phenomena can eventually be deconstructed into physical processes, even if those processes may vary across different physical entities.

In the realm of artificial intelligence and machine consciousness, reductive physicalism finds fascinating applications. If mental states can indeed be reduced to physical states, it implies that creating machines with consciousness is theoretically feasible. By replicating the complex neural configurations and biochemical interactions of the human brain in artificial substrates, we might one day achieve machine consciousness. This raises profound ethical and philosophical questions about the nature of mind, identity, and technology that defy easy answers but affirm the interconnectedness of mind and body within the reductive physicalist framework.

Furthermore, the intersection of reductive physicalism with religious thought presents both opportunities and tensions. Many religious traditions privilege the soul or spirit as distinct from the body, a view diametrically opposed to reductive physicalism. Roman Catholic theology, for example, emphasizes the spiritual dimensions of human life, often in ways that resist reduction to mere physicality. However, some theologians argue that God's creation includes the physical laws and structures discovered by science, which can work harmoniously with spiritual beliefs. Bridging these two realms requires more dialogue and nuanced understanding to reconcile faith with scientific insights.

In conclusion, reductive physicalism offers a robust explanatory framework for understanding consciousness by anchoring mental phenomena in physical processes. While it successfully integrates findings from neuroscience and addresses long-standing philosophical queries about the mind-body relationship, it is not without substantial challenges. The subjective nature of experience, ethical concerns related to AI, and the dialogue between science and religion all continue to provoke critical examination of reductive physicalism's scope and limits. Future advancements in multiple disciplines will likely shape the contours of this ongoing intellectual adventure.

Non-reductive Physicalism

Non-reductive physicalism occupies a unique space within the broader landscape of physicalist theories. This standpoint accepts that everything is ultimately grounded in physical states and processes, yet it denies that mental states can be fully reduced to physical properties. In other words, non-reductive physicalism maintains a physicalist ontology, but it recognizes the autonomy of the mental.

At its core, non-reductive physicalism asserts that mental properties emerge from but are not reducible to physical properties. This view stands in contrast to reductive physicalism, which seeks to explain mental phenomena entirely in terms of physical processes. The autonomy of mental properties is upheld by the claim that these properties can have causal powers of their own, independent of their physical bases. For instance, mental states such as beliefs or desires can cause physical actions, a concept often referred to as "mental causation" (Kim, 1998).

One important aspect of non-reductive physicalism is its commitment to multiple realizability. This principle posits that the same mental state can be realized by different physical states across diverse organisms. A mental state like pain, for instance, might be instantiated by different neural configurations in humans, octopuses, or even hypothetical artificial intelligences. This indicates that mental states can't be neatly reduced to particular physical states, due to their varied realizations across different substrates (Putnam, 1975).

Non-reductive physicalism also engages deeply with the philosophy of mind, particularly through discussions on supervenience. Supervenience is the idea that mental properties depend on physical properties in such a way that any change in a mental property must correspond to a change in the underlying physical property. Yet, this neither entails a reduction nor an identity between the properties. Thus, while mental properties are contingent on the physical, they maintain a distinct existence with unique causal roles (Davidson, 1970).

A frequent challenge to non-reductive physicalism rests in addressing the causal exclusion problem. The crux of this problem lies in explaining how mental properties can have genuine causal efficacy without being redundant, given that physical properties are causally sufficient. Critics argue that if every physical effect has a sufficient physical cause, then the causal work done by mental properties appears superfluous. Non-reductive physicalists often respond by emphasizing that mental properties bring a different kind of causal power into play, one that can't be overridden by purely physical descriptions (Block, 2003).

The debate around qualia and phenomenal experience also weighs heavily on non-reductive physicalism. Qualia refer to the subjective, qualitative aspects of conscious experience—the "what it is like" to experience something. Non-reductive physicalists acknowledge these phenomena without resorting to dualism. They argue that while qualia are indeed emergent properties dependent on physical states, they possess unique phenomenological characteristics that resist reductive explanations (Chalmers, 1996).

Neuroscience often intersects with these philosophical discussions, particularly in exploring the neural correlates of consciousness (NCCs). Non-reductive physicalism doesn't deny the importance of NCCs but asserts that understanding them fully requires moving beyond reductive accounts. The neural basis provides the substrate, yet the emergent mental experiences must be considered within their own realm of discourse. This is akin to how understanding the chemical properties of water doesn't wholly capture the wetness we experience (Crick & Koch, 2003).

In theological contexts, non-reductive physicalism offers a middle ground that can be appealing. By maintaining that mental states and conscious experiences are rooted in the physical, it remains consistent with scientific understandings. Simultaneously, by preserving the autonomy and unique properties of the mental, it echoes religious and spiritual intuitions about the soul, mind, and human dignity. This can provide fertile ground for dialogue between science and religion, as it respects the methodologies and insights of both (Murphy, 2006).

Philosophically, non-reductive physicalism aligns well with emergentism, which argues that higher-level complex phenomena originate from foundational physical systems but aren't directly reducible to them. This view suggests a bottom-up construction wherein intricate structures yield novel properties, maintaining consistency with a physicalist framework even as it accounts for the richness and complexity of mental life (O'Connor & Wong, 2005).

It's essential to recognize that non-reductive physicalism is not without its detractors. Critics often point out that delineating precisely how mental properties can exhibit causal powers without violating physicalist principles remains a contentious terrain. Moreover, the exact nature of the relationship between mental states and their physical substrates continues to evoke debates, with some arguing that non-reductive physicalism doesn't fully escape the pitfalls of dualism.

However, supporters of non-reductive physicalism argue that this position provides a coherent and pragmatic approach to understanding consciousness. It preserves a respect for scientific inquiry into the physical foundations of mental states while also acknowledging the irreducible complexity of qualitative, subjective experience. This dual recognition enables a more nuanced and comprehensive exploration of human consciousness, one that accommodates both empirical findings and phenomenological richness.

In summary, non-reductive physicalism represents a robust and versatile framework within physicalist theories of mind. By upholding the ontological primacy of the physical while insisting on the emergent and irreducible nature of mental states, it opens pathways for interdisciplinary dialogue and advances our understanding of consciousness's multifaceted nature.

Challenges to Physicalism

Physicalism, the view that everything about the mind can be explained in physical terms, stands as a dominant force in contemporary philosophy of mind and cognitive science. Despite its intuitive appeal and the support it garners from advancements in neuroscience, physicalism faces several robust challenges. These objections come from various quarters—philosophical, empirical, and theological—making it imperative to examine the most compelling critiques.

One of the foremost philosophical challenges to physicalism is the "explanatory gap" identified by Thomas Nagel and further elaborated by Joseph Levine (Nagel, 1974; Levine, 1983). The explanatory gap question highlights that physicalist accounts often fail to bridge the divide between physical processes and subjective experiences, or qualia. For instance, knowing everything about the brain's workings and the behavior it produces doesn't inherently explain why we experience the color red as we do. This gap intimates that there might be an aspect of consciousness that physical explanations inherently cannot capture.

In line with the explanatory gap, we encounter the "hard problem of consciousness," famously articulated by David Chalmers (Chalmers, 1995). While physicalism may successfully address the "easy problems" of cognition, such as explaining behaviors and brain functions, it struggles to elucidate why and how these processes are accompanied by subjective experiences. This hard problem emphasizes the apparent insufficiency of purely physical explanations to account for the richness of human interiority.

A related challenge comes from Frank Jackson's thought experiment known as the "knowledge argument" or "Mary's Room" (Jackson, 1982). Jackson imagines a brilliant scientist, Mary, who knows all there is to know about the neurophysiology of color vision but has never experienced color herself due to living in a black-and-white room. Upon experiencing color for the first time, Mary learns something new—what it is like to see color—suggesting that there are non-physical aspects to consciousness that escape even the most complete physical accounts.

While these philosophical challenges point to the potential incompleteness of physicalist explanations, empirical challenges stem from the limits of contemporary neuroscience. Although significant progress has been made in understanding the neural correlates of consciousness, a complete and unified theory explaining how neural processes give rise to subjective experiences remains elusive. The complexity of brain functions, alongside individual variability, poses a significant empirical hurdle to realizing the physicalist vision in scientific terms (Crick & Koch, 1990).

Additionally, there are compelling theological objections to physicalism. For many religious traditions, consciousness and the soul are more than just physical entities. Theological views often posit that consciousness serves as a bridge to the transcendent, carrying moral and spiritual significance that physicalism struggles to account for. The Catholic Church, for instance, views the human person as a union of body and soul, where the soul has intrinsic value and immortality that cannot be reduced to physical processes (Ratzinger, 1995). This metaphysical commitment inherently challenges the physicalist framework, which cannot accommodate non-physical entities like an immortal soul.

Ethical and existential challenges further complicate the picture for physicalism. If consciousness and, by extension, personhood are reducible to physical processes, questions arise concerning free will, moral responsibility, and personal identity. Physicalism can seemingly lead to a determinist outlook where human behavior is merely the product of neural firings and biochemical reactions. Such a perspective can undermine notions of moral agency and accountability, raising thorny questions about justice and human dignity (Dennett, 2003).

Moreover, personal identity under a physicalist framework faces significant issues. The continuity of personal identity, essential for concepts like moral responsibility and the self, becomes challenging to maintain if we are merely collections of changing physical states. Philosophers like Derek Parfit have argued that if personal identity is not about a single continuous entity but rather a series of connected psychological states, then the physicalist account strips away the unique sense of self that many find intuitively compelling and existentially important (Parfit, 1984).

To compound these challenges, alternative theories of mind, such as panpsychism and emergentism, offer resilient counterpoints. Panpsychism, for instance, posits that consciousness is a fundamental and ubiquitous feature of the universe, embedded in even the simplest forms of matter. This perspective circumvents some of the explanatory gaps faced by physicalism by positing that consciousness doesn't arise from complex arrangements of matter but is a basic constituent of reality (Strawson, 2006). Similarly, emergentism suggests that while mental states arise from physical processes, they possess properties and causal powers that are irreducible to those processes. This offers a middle ground that maintains the physical basis of consciousness while acknowledging its unique, emergent features (Kim, 1999).

While the challenges to physicalism are diverse and multifaceted, they share a common thread: they question whether physicalism alone can adequately account for the richness of conscious experience. The various critiques—from the philosophical and theological to the empirical and ethical—encourage a broader, more nuanced discourse. They call into question whether a solely physicalist ontology can provide a comprehensive understanding of what it means to be conscious, urging us to consider alternative or complementary frameworks.

Indeed, as we push the frontiers of neuroscience and cognitive science, the dialogue between physicalism and its challengers continues to be dynamic and essential. Addressing these challenges requires an openness to interdisciplinary research and a willingness to integrate insights from philosophy, theology, and empirical science. Only through such a holistic approach can we hope to shed more light on the profound mystery of consciousness and its place in the cosmos.

Chapter 10: Alternative Views

In the rich tapestry of consciousness studies, alternative views like panpsychism and emergentism offer compelling frameworks that challenge the dominant paradigms of dualism and physicalism. Panpsychism, positing that consciousness is a fundamental aspect of all matter, invites us to reconsider our anthropocentric biases and speculate on the potential ubiquity of conscious experience in the universe (Chalmers, 1996). Emergentism, on the other hand, proposes that consciousness arises from complex physical interactions yet cannot be entirely reduced to these components, underscoring the limitations of reductionist approaches (Bedau, 1997). These perspectives not only provide fertile ground for reimagining the mind-body problem, but also force us to question the very nature of reality itself, offering new pathways to bridge the gaps between theology, science, and philosophy in understanding consciousness.

Panpsychism

Among the myriad theories proposed to explain the nature of consciousness, panpsychism stands out for its audacity and simplicity. In essence, panpsychism posits that consciousness is a fundamental and ubiquitous feature of the universe. Unlike dualism, which separates mind and matter, and physicalism, which seeks to reduce consciousness to physical processes, panpsychism asserts that consciousness exists at all levels of reality. It suggests that even the most basic entities in the universe possess some form of subjective experience.

At its core, panpsychism challenges the very foundation of traditional Western metaphysical assumptions. It offers a radical rethinking of the way we approach the mind-body problem, essentially bridging the mental and the physical by infusing all matter with a mental aspect. Proponents argue that if we accept the existence of consciousness in higher forms like humans, it becomes easier to envision a spectrum of consciousness that pervades all matter, albeit in much simpler forms (Goff, 2019).

Philosophically, traces of panpsychist thought can be found in ancient traditions. Various forms of animism, which attribute life and spirit to natural elements like rivers, mountains, and trees, can be viewed as early expressions of panpsychism. The pre-Socratic philosopher Thales is often cited for his assertion that "everything is full of gods," indicating a belief in a pervasive, essential consciousness (Seager, 2006).

Modern panpsychism finds its roots in more recent philosophical inquiry, notably in the works of thinkers like Leibniz and Spinoza. Leibniz's monadology, with its notion of simple substances or "monads" as fundamental units of reality imbued with perception, aligns closely with panpsychist ideas. Spinoza's pantheism, which identifies God with the totality of the universe, also echoes panpsychist principles by suggesting a form of universal consciousness (Strawson, 2006).

In contemporary discussions, panpsychism has gained traction as a viable alternative to both dualism and physicalism. One of its most vocal advocates, philosopher Philip Goff, argues that panpsychism offers a more coherent solution to the "hard problem" of consciousness—the question of how and why physical processes produce subjective experiences (Goff, 2019). According to panpsychism, the hard problem dissolves because consciousness is not an emergent property to be explained; rather, it is a fundamental feature of the universe.

From a scientific perspective, panpsychism raises intriguing questions but also faces significant hurdles. While it elegantly sidesteps some of the common pitfalls associated with physicalist reductionism, it remains challenging to empirically validate. Modern neuroscience, deeply entrenched in a physicalist paradigm, finds it difficult to accommodate a theory that implies consciousness at subatomic levels. Critics argue that without clear empirical evidence, panpsychism risks veering into speculative metaphysics rather than remaining grounded in rigorous scientific inquiry (Chalmers, 1996).

Nonetheless, some scientists have begun to explore interdisciplinary approaches that might lend credence to panpsychism. Integrated Information Theory (IIT), for instance, developed by neuroscientist Giulio Tononi, aims to mathematically quantify consciousness. IIT suggests that any system with integrated information possesses consciousness to some degree, a concept that resonates with panpsychist principles (Tononi, 2008). While IIT does not explicitly endorse panpsychism, it opens the door to scientific models that do not entirely dismiss the idea of a ubiquitous consciousness.

From a theological and philosophical standpoint, panpsychism offers a platform for reconciling spirituality with scientific inquiry. Religious traditions that espouse the interconnectedness of all life, such as certain strands of Hinduism and Buddhism, naturally align with panpsychist ideas. Roman Catholic thought, particularly in its emphasis on the sanctity and unity of creation, might find a surprising kinship with panpsychism, though this alignment is not without its challenges. Theologically, embracing panpsychism requires a shift from anthropocentric views of consciousness to a more holistic understanding of divine presence in the universe (Haught, 1995).

In the realm of psychiatry, the implications of panpsychism are tantalizing yet complex. If consciousness is indeed a fundamental aspect of even the smallest particles, this could reshape our understanding of mental health and illness. Traditional psychiatric models often rely on a dualistic separation of mind and body or a physicalist focus on biological processes. Panpsychism, by contrast, invites a more integrated approach that considers the mental and physical as inherently connected. This perspective could revolutionize therapeutic practices, fostering treatments that address the holistic nature of human beings.

However, critics of panpsychism caution against over-extending the theory's reach. They argue that without concrete evidence, panpsychism remains speculative and may divert valuable resources and attention from more empirically grounded research avenues. Additionally, the challenge of defining and measuring consciousness in non-human entities, or even in inanimate matter, remains formidable. Philosophical rigor and scientific scrutiny are essential to keeping panpsychism within the bounds of serious scholarly discourse.

In conclusion, panpsychism reimagines consciousness not as an exclusive trait of complex organisms but as a fundamental feature of reality itself. This perspective offers a fresh lens through which to explore the mind-body problem, bringing together insights from philosophy, theology, and science. While it faces substantial criticism and empirical challenges, panpsychism continues to provoke thought and inspire debate among scholars across disciplines. It beckons us to consider the possibility that consciousness is not confined to the realm of the human but permeates the very fabric of the universe.

Chapter 11: Ã¢ÂÂ Historical Background

In delving into the historical background of consciousness, it's crucial to navigate through the complex corridors of intellectual history. The exploration begins with early Greek philosophers. Socrates, Plato, and Aristotle each proposed foundational ideas that would later influence centuries of thought. Socrates' dialogues, carefully penned by Plato, sought to discern the nature of knowledge, virtue, and the soul, hinting at a form of proto-psychology (Plato, 1961).

Plato's theory of the Forms suggested that the true essence of things exists in an abstract realm, separate from the material world. This dualistic perspective laid a cornerstone for later dualist philosophies that see mind and body as distinct entities. Aristotle deviated, emphasizing empirical observation and positing the psyche (soul) as the form of a living being, tightly interwoven with its physical structure (Aristotle, 1991). This divergence would set the stage for enduring debates on the nature of consciousness and its relation to the physical world.

As centuries rolled on, medieval philosophy blended these classical thoughts with theological insights. Augustine of Hippo, a pivotal figure, merged Neoplatonism with Christian doctrine, suggesting that the mind's capacity to know truth indicates its divine nature. Augustine's confessions mirrored a more introspective approach, probing the relationship between human consciousness and God's eternal wisdom (Augustine, 2006).

Moving to the high medieval period, Thomas Aquinas exerted a profound influence with his synthesis of Aristotelian philosophy and Christian theology. Aquinas posited that the soul is the form of the body, but its intellectual component can exist independently, suggesting a form of dualism that respects the unity of human nature. His work remains a linchpin for understanding how medieval thinkers grappled with the mind-body problem (Aquinas, 1920).

The Renaissance and Enlightenment periods marked a seismic shift, emphasizing empirical investigation and human reason. Descartes, often dubbed the father of modern philosophy, reignited dualistic notions with his cogito, ergo sum ("I think, therefore I am"). By positing the mind as a distinct substance from the body, Descartes provided a clear, albeit controversial, framework for subsequent discussions on consciousness (Descartes, 1996).

In stark contrast, Hobbes and Locke offered materialistic counterpoints. Hobbes viewed all mental phenomena as arising from physical processes. Locke, while not rejecting the mind's distinction from the body, emphasized empirical experience as the source of all knowledge, including knowledge of one's own consciousness (Locke, 1975). These perspectives foreshadowed the emergence of physicalist theories that dominate contemporary discourse.

The 19th and early 20th centuries bore witness to further diversification in thought. Hegelian dialectics reintroduced idealism, positing that reality is fundamentally mental or spiritual. Conversely, Marxist materialism grounded consciousness in socio-economic conditions, eschewing spiritual or idealist interpretations.

Sigmund Freud, with his groundbreaking psychoanalytic theory, mapped the unconscious mind, attributing complex behaviors to hidden, often primitive impulses and unresolved conflicts. Freud's model revolutionized psychology, blending Victorian scientific rigor with a novel introspective depth (Freud, 2010).

William James, a towering figure in American psychology, approached consciousness with pragmatism. His "stream of consciousness" metaphor illustrated the fluid, ever-changing nature of human experience. James' contributions laid groundwork that remains influential, particularly in phenomenological and existential psychology (James, 1890).

As we enter the 20th century, phenomenology and existentialism introduced fresh lenses for examining consciousness. Edmund Husserl's phenomenology sought to rigorously describe experiences from the first-person perspective, pioneering methods that eschew the reduction of consciousness to mere physical processes (Husserl, 1913). Simultaneously, existentialists like Jean-Paul Sartre emphasized the centrality of human freedom and subjectivity, arguing that consciousness is always consciousness of something, thus establishing an intentional structure to human experience (Sartre, 1943).

The quantum leaps in neuroscience, spurred by advances in technology, have grounded modern debates in empirical evidence. Neuroimaging and electrophysiological studies provide unprecedented insights into brain activity, correlating specific neural patterns with conscious experiences. These advancements challenge and refine earlier philosophical positions, demanding an interdisciplinary approach for a holistic understanding of consciousness.

In examining these historical perspectives, we observe a tapestry of thought, with frequent oscillations between dualistic and monistic interpretations. Each era, informed by its unique cultural, scientific, and theological contexts, contributed nuanced insights that continue to shape contemporary discussions. Understanding this background equips us to better appreciate and engage with the multifaceted debates on the nature of consciousness that unfold in subsequent chapters.

Chapter 12: Ã¢ÂÂ Contemporary Theories

The contemporary landscape of consciousness studies is marked by a rich tapestry of theories that strive to bridge the elusive gap between mind and matter. Among the most compelling are emergentism, which posits that consciousness arises from complex system interactions yet is not reducible to mere physical components, and panpsychism, which argues that consciousness is a fundamental aspect of all matter. These modern theoretical frameworks offer an alternative to traditional dualistic and physicalist paradigms, suggesting that consciousness could be a property emerging from the intricate networking of simpler entities. While emergentism finds its roots in the hierarchical complexity of biological systems (Kim, 2006), panpsychism extends its reach to suggest that even the simplest particles possess proto-conscious properties (Goff et al., 2017). These theories challenge us to rethink the nature of consciousness through a multidisciplinary lens, integrating insights from neuroscience, philosophy, and computational theory. As such, contemporary approaches do not just complement older theories but also seek to resolve lingering paradoxes by proposing more integrative and dynamic models (Chalmers, 2010).

Emergentism

The theory of emergentism has intrigued philosophers, scientists, and theologians alike due to its compelling proposition: consciousness arises from physical processes yet cannot be fully reduced to them. Emergentism navigates the middle ground between dualism and physicalism by suggesting that new properties can 'emerge' from complex systems that aren't wholly explainable through their individual components.

Emergentism's roots can be traced back to the early 20th century, gaining traction through philosophers such as C.D. Broad and later, Jaegwon Kim, who have extensively explored how mental states can emerge from brain states (Broad, 1925; Kim, 1999). This theory posits that while the mind is grounded in the physical substrate of the brain, it cannot be exhaustively understood in terms of purely physical processes. This is because the emergent properties possess new causal powers that aren't present in the constituent parts alone (O'Connor & Wong, 2015).

One of the most alluring aspects of emergentism is its alignment with certain scientific principles, particularly those observed in complex systems and biology. Consider consciousness akin to a hurricane: while a hurricane is the result of specific atmospheric conditions, understanding wind speed and temperature alone doesn't wholly clarify the phenomenon of the hurricane itself. Similarly, while neuronal activity underpins conscious experience, understanding the activity of individual neurons alone may not fully explain the subjective experience (Laughlin, 2005).

In contemporary discussions, emergentism gains significance as a viable alternative to both reductive physicalism and substance dualism. Reductive physicalism often struggles to account for the rich tapestry of qualia—that is, the subjective character of experience—without seeming to lose the essence of experience itself. Substance dualism, while maintaining the qualitative aspect of consciousness, proposes a metaphysical chasm between mind and matter that feels increasingly anachronistic in light of modern scientific findings. Emergentism, thus, endeavors to synthesize an appreciation for both the qualitative and quantitative elements of consciousness.

Emergent properties are, in various ways, dependent on their foundational structures but introduce new causal capacities. Consciousness, viewed from this angle, emerges from the neural substrate but embodies unique characteristics not reducible to individual neuronal activities. It's akin to how wetness emerges from the interaction of water molecules, even though no single molecule possesses this property alone. This emergent property approach provides a nuanced understanding that avoids the pitfalls of reducing mental states to mere brain states (Clayton, 2004).

Crucially, emergentism also opens pathways to reconcile some theological concepts with scientific understanding. For instance, the idea of the soul could be conceptualized as an emergent property of the brain, rather than an entirely separate entity. This aligns with views held in some contemporary Roman Catholic theological circles, where the soul and body are seen as deeply interwoven rather than entirely distinct (Ratzinger, 2005). In such a framework, divine interaction with human souls could be interpreted as interacting with these highly complex, emergent systems—an interpretation that adds a layer of profundity to religious beliefs about human nature.

Moreover, emergentism can be pivotal in psychiatric and psychological practice. If mental disorders like depression or schizophrenia are seen as emergent phenomena, then treatment could benefit from a holistic approach, integrating pharmacological and therapeutic interventions. The emergent properties of consciousness and mental states imply that changes at the neuronal level can manifest in profound psychological shifts, and vice versa (Sloman, 2000).

Emergentism's implications extend into moral and ethical realms as well. By grounding subjective experiences in emergent properties, moral and ethical considerations gain a more substantial anchorage. The intrinsic value of human experiences and the moral weight attributed to individual suffering are underscored, compelling society to examine ethical frameworks more pointedly.

Critics, however, question whether emergent properties can genuinely offer new causative forces or if they merely reflect our inability to comprehend complex systems fully. They argue that claiming 'emergence' without concrete mechanistic explanations risks veering into mysticism or hand-waving (Kim, 2006). Such criticisms call for rigorous explanatory models demonstrating how emergent properties arise and exert causal influence.

Despite these critiques, research in neuroscience continues to unveil layers of complexity within brain function that bolster the emergentist perspective. Advanced imaging technologies and computational models offer insights into how large-scale neural networks might give rise to emergent properties such as consciousness (Tononi, 2012). These scientific strides hint at a future where emergent properties are not merely philosophical postulates but empirically validated phenomena.

Emergentism, therefore, stands as a promising territory for interdisciplinary exploration. Its ability to bridge gaps between hard sciences, philosophy, and theology makes it uniquely poised to deepen our understanding of consciousness. As we continue to unravel the complexities of the brain and consciousness, emergentism provides a flexible yet robust framework to investigate questions that have fascinated humanity for millennia.

Chapter 13: Ã¢ÂÂ Varieties of Emergence

Emergence, in the context of the mind-body problem, presents a captivating puzzle as it lies at the confluence of theology, science, and philosophy. In its broadest sense, emergence refers to the process by which novel properties, patterns, or behaviors arise from the interactions among simpler components in a system. This chapter seeks to disentangle the various strands of emergence, examining how they contribute to our understanding of consciousness. By delving into these varieties, we aim to clarify how complex mental states can arise from physical substrates.

First, let's consider strong emergence. Advocates argue that emergent properties possess causal powers independent of their constituent parts. For instance, consciousness could be seen as possessing powers that are not reducible to neural activities or any other physical processes. This perspective often resonates with those inclined towards dualism, as it suggests a kind of ontological novelty exclusive to mental phenomena. From a theological standpoint, strong emergence aligns well with the notion of the soul as an entity interacting with yet distinct from the physical body. The resistance of strong emergence to reductive explanations provides a platform where both philosophical and theological narratives can intersect (Chalmers, 2006).

On the other hand, weak emergence posits that emergent properties are merely unpredictable based on our current understanding of the system's constituents but are ultimately reducible to these components. This view finds favor among many physicalists who argue that, albeit complex, consciousness can be wholly understood through the study of neural processes and interactions. From a scientific perspective, weak emergence seems more palatable because it adheres to the principle of causal closure in the physical world. The brain's complexity might obscure our understanding, but it doesn't necessitate the introduction of non-physical entities or properties.

Now consider the notion of downward causation, an essential concept in the discussion of emergence. Downward causation implies that higher-level phenomena (like consciousness) can exert causal influence on lower-level processes (like neural activities). This concept is contentious. While it suggests a more integrative approach to understanding the mind-body relationship, critics argue it might conflict with well-established physical laws (Kim, 1999). If higher-level mental properties can influence the lower-level physical states, does this not contravene the causal closure of the physical domain? This dilemma remains one of the thorniest issues in the exploration of emergent consciousness.

The context of complex systems also contributes significantly to our understanding of emergent phenomena. Consider the emergent behavior in flocks of birds or schools of fish. Each bird or fish follows simple rules, yet the resulting movement appears sophisticated and coordinated. Drawing an analogy with consciousness, proponents argue that individual neurons obey relatively simple rules, but their collective behavior gives rise to the richness of conscious experience. This parallel invites a more interdisciplinary approach, incorporating insights from fields like biology, physics, and even computer science to decode the mysteries of consciousness (Mitchell, 2009).

Philosophically, emergence hails back to the Aristotelian notion of "the whole being greater than the sum of its parts," yet its modern interpretation is heavily influenced by developments in complexity science and systems theory. Emergent properties often seem to be context-dependent, arising from the specific arrangement and interaction of components. Therefore, the epistemological challenge is to understand how these interactions translate into higher-order properties. Here, the fine line between epistemology and ontology blurs, posing questions about the very nature of reality and our capacity to comprehend it.

Emergent properties might also be classified based on their dependency relationships. Constitutive emergence implies that the whole's properties are fundamentally dependent on its parts and their interactions. However, contextual emergence suggests these properties only come into being under specific contextual constraints. For instance, a single neuron doesn't exhibit the property of memory, but networks of neurons under particular conditions can indeed encode and retrieve memories. This view encourages an appreciation of the contextual factors and environmental constraints that play crucial roles in the emergence of mental phenomena.

The study of artificial intelligence (AI) offers another intriguing arena for exploring emergent phenomena. As we design increasingly complex neural networks, some argue these systems exhibit primitive forms of consciousness or cognition. While skeptical voices caution against anthropomorphizing AI, the field nevertheless provides valuable insights into how complex behaviors and properties emerge from simple algorithms and vast datasets. This convergence of artificial intelligence and emergentism underscores the non-linear, often unpredictable trajectories through which complexity and novel properties arise.

The ethical considerations of emergentism cannot be ignored either. If consciousness is seen as an emergent property of complex neural activities, it raises profound questions about the moral status of non-human entities exhibiting similar emergent properties. Can we extend notions of personhood and moral rights to advanced AI or other forms of synthetic life? This quandary necessitates a re-examination of our ethical frameworks, urging us to consider the broader implications of emergent consciousness in our technological age (Floridi et al., 2018).

The theological implications of emergentism are equally rich. If we consider human consciousness as an emergent property within God's created order, how does this influence our understanding of divine interaction with the world? Does it imply a more immanent view of God's relationship with creation, mirroring the way emergent properties arise from physical substrates? Or does it suggest a dual-aspect monism, where both physical and mental properties are two aspects of a more fundamental reality? These reflections invite deeper contemplation on how theological doctrines harmonize with scientific discoveries about emergence.

In conclusion, the varieties of emergence offer a multifaceted lens through which to examine consciousness. Whether approached from a perspective of strong or weak emergence, considering the implications of downward causation, or exploring parallels in complex systems and AI, the study of emergence challenges and enriches our understanding of the mind-body problem. The delicate interplay between the parts and the whole, between the physical and the mental, underscores the complexity of consciousness. As we continue to probe these depths, we must remain cognizant of the interdisciplinary and often paradoxical nature of the journey.

Chapter 14: Ã¢Â□Â□ Empirical Support

Empirical evidence provides the bedrock upon which scientific theories stand or fall. Over the years, a multitude of studies have endeavored to bridge the chasm between the subjective experience of consciousness and its physical underpinnings. This chapter focuses on the empirical support for various theories of consciousness such as dualism, physicalism, panpsychism, and emergentism, while carefully considering the intricate interplay between them. Through meticulous examination of case studies, experiments, and neurological findings, we uncover the nuanced reality of the mind-body problem.

Empirical support for dualism may initially appear tenuous, yet there are compelling instances in clinical settings that beg for attention. Take, for example, the phenomena surrounding near-death experiences (NDEs). Some patients undergoing cardiac arrest have reported vivid experiences during periods of brain inactivity that challenge a purely physicalist explanation of consciousness (Parnia et al., 2001). These experiences often include memories, emotions, and visions that suggest a form of consciousness independent of the brain's functions, adding weight to dualistic theories.

In contrast, physicalism garners extensive empirical support through brain imaging technologies like fMRI and PET scans, which reveal how specific neural activities correlate with conscious experiences. For example, research has demonstrated that the posterior hot zone of the brain is closely associated with the content of visual experiences (Koch et al., 2016). By mapping these neural correlates of consciousness, scientists furnish concrete evidence that supports the physicalist position, positing that consciousness arises from brain activity.

Yet, the conversation is far from one-dimensional. Emergentism, which asserts that consciousness is an emergent property of complex systems, benefits from empirical support drawn from systems biology and network theory. Studies in artificial intelligence and complex systems indicate that higher-order properties often arise unpredictably from simpler interactions (Mitchell, 2009). For instance, the emergent behavior of a flock of birds or the intricate synchronization of neurons present compelling analogies for understanding how consciousness might emerge from non-conscious components.

The empirical scrutiny extends to panpsychism, a theory most skeptics find audacious yet intriguing. Although panpsychism claims that consciousness is a fundamental feature of all matter, empirical validation is more abstract. Researchers often point to quantum mechanics and properties of fundamental particles, yet the evidence remains deeply theoretical rather than observable. However, an increasing number of physicists and philosophers argue that phenomena like quantum entanglement indicate that even inert matter could possess proto-consciousness (Goff, 2019).

The landmark experiments on split-brain patients also offer invaluable empirical data, providing critical insights into the mind-matter relationship. When the corpus callosum is severed, patients exhibit dual cognitive processes, as though two minds inhabit a single body. This phenomenon resonates with both dualist and multi-faceted physicalist interpretations. On one hand, it suggests the possibility of multiple conscious entities within one brain, aligning somewhat with dualist views. On the other hand, it underscores how physical alterations can fragment consciousness, providing a strong case for physicalism (Gazzaniga, 2005).

Neuroplasticity also enriches our discussion by showcasing the brain's ability to reorganize itself, thus challenging static views of consciousness. Empirical studies demonstrate that the brain's structure and function can change significantly in response to experiences, injuries, or training, suggesting that consciousness is not only a product of brain activity but also adaptable (Doidge, 2007). This capacity for change simultaneously supports non-reductive physicalism and emergentism, as it highlights how consciousness can evolve from complex interactions within a malleable system.

Furthermore, empirical support for consciousness theories benefits from advancements in computational neuroscience. Models simulating neural networks provide a sandbox for testing hypotheses about consciousness emergence, bridging theoretical assumptions and observable phenomena. Projects like the Blue Brain Project aim to recreate the neural architecture of the human brain in silico, providing platforms for experiments that would be impossible in biological settings (Markram, 2006).

In sum, empirical support for consciousness theories spans a broad spectrum, replete with compelling data and thought-provoking phenomena. By examining neural correlates, split-brain cases, and the adaptive nature of neuroplasticity, alongside theoretical constructs from quantum mechanics and emergent systems, we gain a multi-faceted understanding of this elusive subject.

Empirical evidence does not conclude the debate but opens new avenues for inquiry. Each theory — dualism, physicalism, panpsychism, and emergentism — finds anchorage in the tangible world, albeit to varying extents. As our scientific tools and methodologies evolve, so too will the clarity with which we understand consciousness, bridging gaps between philosophy, theology, and empirical science.

Chapter 15: Reconciling Theology with Science

In attempting to reconcile theology with science, one faces the monumental task of bridging two realms historically considered at odds. Theology, rooted in divine revelation and metaphysical speculation, often appears to stand in contrast to the empirical and methodical nature of scientific inquiry. Yet, both domains seek to elucidate the mysteries of human consciousness and existence. From Thomas Aquinas' assertion of the harmony between reason and faith to contemporary dialogues in neurotheology, which study the neural correlates of spiritual experiences, there is a growing acknowledgment that these fields enrich rather than contradict each other. While scientific studies reveal the brain's intricate processes during religious experiences (Newberg et al., 2001), theologians interpret these findings through the lens of divine immanence and transcendence. For instance, the neural activation observed in meditative states, such as heightened activity in the prefrontal cortex, correlates with the sense of unity and peace described in mystical traditions (Davidson & Lutz, 2008). Reconciling these perspectives requires a nuanced understanding that neither diminishes the role of divine agency nor discredits the validity of empirical observations. By fostering interdisciplinary dialogue, one may arrive at a more holistic understanding of human consciousness that respects both scientific rigor and theological depth.

Religious Perspectives on the Mind

The intertwining of theological doctrines and scientific inquiry offers a rich tapestry for exploring the nature of the mind. From the halls of religious academia to the sanctuaries of faith, religious perspectives on the mind illuminate a dimension of human experience that scientific paradigms often struggle to grapple with fully. It's imperative to recognize that religious traditions have long engaged with questions of consciousness, identity, and the soul, often predating modern scientific frameworks.

In Christianity, one foundational perspective roots the mind within the soul, a divine creation open to participation in the mystery of the divine. The mind isn't seen merely as a byproduct of physical processes but as an essential element of a person's spiritual nature. From St. Augustine to Thomas Aquinas, Christian thought has grappled with the dual aspects of human existence—material and immaterial. Aquinas, for example, integrated Aristotelian philosophy with Christian theology to argue that the soul is the form of the body, but it possesses faculties such as intellect and will that surpass mere physical explanation (Aquinas, 2005).

Judaism too accommodates a complex view of the mind. The Hebrew term "nefesh" often gets translated as "soul," although its meaning spans the breadth of life force, individuality, and inner life. Rabbinic literature and mystical traditions like Kabbalah examine the mind not merely as a component of human nature but as an apparatus for divine interaction. The mind in Jewish thought is capable of elevating ordinary life to divine service. The principle of "Tikkun Olam," or repairing the world, places an onus on mental faculties both for self-improvement and communal harmony (Idel, 1988).

Islam offers yet another layer of understanding. The Qur'an speaks of the "nafs," or self, drawing a distinction between its base desires and higher spiritual aspirations. The mind in Islamic thought navigates these planes, remaining central to the human pursuit of divine knowledge and ethical living. Sufi traditions, in particular, provide intricate maps for understanding the mind's role in mystical experiences and spiritual enlightenment. Ibn al-Arabi, a seminal figure in Sufism, proposed that the mind's ultimate aim is to transcend the illusory self and unite with the divine reality (Chittick, 1989).

In the Eastern religious traditions, perspectives diverge but share a common theme in elevating consciousness as a vital aspect of spiritual practice. Hinduism introduces the concept of "Atman," sometimes likened to the soul or self, which transcends individual identity and merges with the universal consciousness, known as "Brahman." Mental faculties in this worldview are both binding and liberating. Practices like yoga aim to purify the mind, reducing the noise generated by transient desires, thus facilitating an alignment with the ultimate reality (Eliade, 2009).

Buddhism also interrogates the nature of the mind but does so through the lens of impermanence and non-self (anatta). The mind, in Buddhist thought, is not an enduring entity but a flow of experiences and mental states, each interdependent and transient. Meditation practices such as Vipassana seek to explore and understand the nature of mind by observing it in real-time. Understanding the mind's impermanent nature is central to achieving enlightenment, which in Buddhism is the cessation of suffering through the realization of ultimate truths (Davids, 1997).

These religious perspectives offer more than theological enrichment; they provide insights that resonate with scientific approaches to understanding the mind. The contemplative practices prevalent in many religious traditions offer empirical data through subjective experiences, akin to phenomenological methods in psychology. For instance, studies have shown that meditation can bring about significant changes in brain function and structure. This opens a dialogue between neuroscience and spiritual practice, showing that religious exercises may have quantifiable effects on mental health and cognition (Davidson et al., 2003).

For Roman Catholics, the ensoulment perspective fosters an enriched dialogue with science, especially in the context of the ever-progressing study of the brain. Pope John Paul II, in his 1996 address to the Pontifical Academy of Sciences, acknowledged that evolution is "more than just a hypothesis" but also affirmed that the soul is a divine gift. This dual recognition promotes a compatibility wherein theological perspectives on the mind and scientific findings on brain development coalesce rather than conflict (John Paul II, 1996).

Moreover, religious experiences themselves often bring forth tangible interactions between theology and psychology. Mystical experiences, visions, and spiritual ecstasies have been subjects of both theological study and psychological examination. William James, a pioneering psychologist, framed religious experiences as integral to understanding the human psyche, thus emphasizing that these events, often relegated to the realm of theology, warrant serious scientific scrutiny (James, 1902).

In summary, religious perspectives on the mind offer dense, multifaceted viewpoints that enrich the discourse surrounding the mind-body problem. They contribute existential dimensions, propose routes for inner development, and present possibilities for compatibility with scientific analyses of consciousness. By embracing these perspectives, skeptics, Roman Catholics, psychiatrists, and academics alike may uncover integrative ways of understanding one of humanity's most enigmatic features—the mind.

Compatibility of Theology and Neuroscience

As we delve into the compatibility of theology and neuroscience, it becomes imperative to recognize that both fields, despite seemingly divergent methodologies and foundational premises, can offer complementary insights into the nature of consciousness. Theology, with its rich tapestry of metaphysical interpretations and doctrines, seeks to understand the divine and the soul's relationship to the body. Neuroscience, grounded firmly in empirical observation and experimentation, strives to unravel the complexities of the brain and its correlation to mental phenomena. The reconciliation of these domains can provide a holistic view that respects both spiritual and scientific dimensions.

Theological perspectives have long held sway in shaping our understanding of consciousness. From the soul's eternal nature in Christian doctrine to the intricate discussions of the mind-body relationship by medieval scholastics, theology offers a framework that addresses questions of ultimate meaning and purpose. For instance, the Roman Catholic tradition, articulated through its magisterium, posits that the human soul is immortal and distinct yet intimately connected to the body (Catechism of the Catholic Church, 1993). This dual aspect resonates well with certain dualistic theories in philosophy which maintain that mental and physical substances are fundamentally different.

However, dualism is not the only lens through which theology can be viewed in light of neuroscience. Emergentist perspectives in theology suggest that while the soul or mind may arise from the physical substrate of the brain, it possesses properties that are not reducible to mere neuronal activity. For instance, Nancey Murphy, a proponent of non-reductive physicalism, argues that while humans are physical beings, our conscious experiences are emergent properties that cannot be wholly explained by physical processes alone (Murphy, 1998). This view dovetails nicely with certain neuroscientific observations that suggest consciousness cannot be pinpointed to a single brain region but rather emerges from complex networks of neural activity.

Conversely, neuroscience challenges and enriches theological perspectives by offering detailed insights into brain functions that correlate with conscious experiences. Advancements in neuroimaging techniques such as fMRI and PET scans have allowed us to observe the brain's workings in real-time, revealing neural correlates of phenomena like meditation, prayer, and mystical experiences, which theology often frames in terms of divine interaction or spiritual revelation (Newberg & Waldman, 2009). These observations can lead to a deeper appreciation of how religious experiences manifest in the brain and encourage a dialogue that goes beyond seeing science and religion as adversarial.

Moreover, the burgeoning field of neurotheology attempts to bridge this gap by exploring how spiritual practices impact brain function and overall mental health. Practices such as contemplative prayer and mindfulness meditation have been shown to induce changes in brain structure and function, leading to improvements in emotional regulation, empathy, and stress reduction (Newberg et al., 2001). These findings suggest that spiritual and religious practices, grounded in theological traditions, have tangible benefits that neuroscience can elucidate and validate.

In engaging with these intersections, one must confront the epistemological limitations of both domains. Theology, rooted in faith and doctrinal teachings, often deals with questions beyond empirical validation, such as the existence of God, the nature of the soul, and the meaning of human existence. Neuroscience, on the other hand, relies on observable and measurable data, thriving within the confines of methodological naturalism. To forge meaningful dialogue, it is crucial to acknowledge these boundaries and find common ground where mutual enrichment can occur.

One of the central theological questions is the nature of the soul and its destiny beyond physical death. Neuroscience, while shedding light on the workings of the brain and its cessation at death, does not venture into metaphysical claims about life after death. Yet, theological doctrines, particularly those concerning resurrection and eternal life, offer a hopeful counter-narrative to the finality implied by a purely materialistic viewpoint. Theologians and neuroscientists can engage in fruitful discussions about how experiences near death, and the transformative effects they have on individuals, may point to realities that transcend empirical observation.

Additionally, ethical considerations play a pivotal role in the intersection of theology and neuroscience. Concepts such as free will, moral responsibility, and the nature of personhood are central to both disciplines. For instance, neuroscientific research into brain areas related to decision-making and moral reasoning intersects with theological discussions on human freedom and divine grace. A dialogue between these fields can foster a robust framework for addressing moral questions, emphasizing human dignity while considering the biological underpinnings of behavior.

Importantly, we must also consider the historical context in which theology and science have interacted. The Galileo affair often symbolizes the tension between these domains, but it is essential to recognize that such conflicts are not inevitable. Wisdom from historical figures like Thomas Aquinas, who synthesized Aristotelian philosophy with Christian theology, reminds us of the potential for integration rather than opposition. Contemporary scholars continue this tradition, seeking to harmonize scientific discoveries with theological insights in a manner that enriches both realms.

The future trajectory of reconciling theology with neuroscience holds much promise. As technology advances and our understanding of the brain deepens, theological concepts can be recontextualized in ways that resonate with modern sensibilities. Such an interdisciplinary approach not only humanizes scientific endeavors but also grounds theological reflections in the lived reality of human experience. This synthesis of knowledge can contribute to a more nuanced and comprehensive understanding of consciousness, respecting the mystery and complexity inherent in human nature.

As we stand at the crossroads of theology and neuroscience, it is incumbent upon scholars, religious leaders, and scientists to approach this dialogue with humility, openness, and a willingness to explore uncharted territories. The quest to understand consciousness is, at its core, a pursuit of truth that transcends disciplinary boundaries. By drawing from the wisdom of both theology and neuroscience, we can aspire to a richer, more integrated understanding of the human mind and its place in the cosmos.

Case Studies in Religious Experience

Reconciling theology with science often calls upon the deep reservoir of individual religious experiences. These experiences, varied and complex, provide a bridge between the empirical realm of science and the often intangible domain of theology. Let's delve into specific case studies that reveal the nuances of religious experience and how they contribute to this reconciliation.

One notable case study involves St. Teresa of Ávila, a 16th-century Spanish mystic whose intense spiritual experiences have been documented extensively. Teresa described experiences of profound unity with God which often occurred during states of altered consciousness. Neurotheological studies have examined such accounts, positing that these mystical states can result from specific neural activities (Newberg, 2010). Her vivid descriptions offer rich qualitative data, prompting hypotheses about the brain's role in facilitating deep spiritual experiences.

Another fascinating account is the conversion experience of St. Augustine as narrated in his "Confessions." Augustine's dramatic shift from a life of secular indulgence to one of devout Christianity has been a focal point for both theologians and psychologists. Augustine's experiences of divine intervention have been analyzed to understand the transformative potential of religious experiences. Psychiatrists like William James have found Augustine's descriptions imperative in understanding religious phenomena through psychological frameworks, arguing that these experiences often involve significant changes in one's neural pathways and emotional states (James, 1902).

Similarly, modern case studies emphasize the neurological underpinnings of religious experience. Consider the case of a 45-year-old man who reported profound spiritual experiences during temporal lobe seizures. These experiences included sensations of overwhelming peace and encounters with a divine presence. Neuroimaging revealed that his seizures originated from areas of the brain associated with emotional processing and self-awareness, suggesting a neurobiological basis for his spiritual experiences (Saver & Rabin, 1997). This case supports the hypothesis that the brain has dedicated systems modulating the capacity for religious experience.

Furthermore, the experiences of contemporary individuals who undergo deep meditation practices also provide valuable insights. Consider the case study of Matthieu Ricard, a former biochemist turned Buddhist monk. Extensive studies on Ricard's brain during meditation revealed unusually high levels of gamma waves, which are associated with consciousness and self-awareness. These findings suggest a neuroplasticity aspect, where long-term meditative practice can fundamentally alter brain structure and function, enhancing states that are often reported as transcendental or divine (Lutz et al., 2004).

In an integrative case study, a group of participants from various religious backgrounds were subjected to brain imaging while engaging in prayer or meditation. The results showcased a consistent activation of the prefrontal cortex and deactivation of the parietal lobes, areas associated with focused attention and self-transcendence, respectively. These consistent findings across diverse religious practices suggest that the human brain might be wired for such transcendental experiences, potentially reconciling diverse theological perspectives with a common neurobiological foundation (Beauregard & Paquette, 2006).

The case study of near-death experiences (NDEs) also bridges theology and science. Individuals recounting NDEs frequently describe encounters with a 'bright light,' feelings of peace, and out-of-body experiences. One highly publicized case involves Dr. Eben Alexander, a neurosurgeon who experienced an NDE during a coma caused by bacterial meningitis. Alexander's detailed post-coma spiritual experiences, which he described as vivid encounters with an all-loving divine figure, challenged his previously held scientific beliefs. His case prompted further scientific inquiry into whether such experiences have a biological basis or if they truly touch upon a divine reality (Alexander, 2012).

Conversely, a more skeptical perspective can be seen in the case studies of non-believers who have experienced religious-like phenomena. For instance, the British psychologist Richard Dawkins underwent transcranial magnetic stimulation (TMS) to induce temporary changes in his brain, particularly in regions associated with religious experience. Although Dawkins did not report a spiritual conversion, he noted unusual mental states, suggesting that the brain's religious experiences' circuitry can be modulated experimentally, supporting a neurobiological explanation (Persinger, 1987).

It is essential to recognize that while these case studies examine the neurological aspects of religious experience, theology brings in the intrinsic value and meaning of these experiences. From a theological perspective, such profound experiences transcend mere neurological events; they touch upon the divine interaction with human consciousness. Theologians argue that the value lies not merely in the occurrence of these experiences but in what they reveal about the ultimate reality and the human relationship with the divine.

The analysis of these case studies underscores an interdisciplinary approach. Neuroscientists, theologians, and philosophers must work collaboratively. Neuroscientists decode the brain's complexity; theologians interpret the divine significance; philosophers weave these interpretations into broader existential inquiries.

In conclusion, these varied case studies in religious experience create a tapestry illustrating the intricate interplay between brain function and spiritual phenomena. They reinforce the idea that reconciling theology and science is not merely possible but essential to fully understanding the phenomena that continue to define the human search for meaning and transcendence.

Chapter 16: Philosophical Implications

The confluence of free will and determinism sits at the heart of the philosophical discourse on consciousness, teasing apart the enigma of whether our choices are genuine acts of volition or mere epiphenomena of neural processes. Personal identity, too, is deeply intertwined with these inquiries, prompting questions about what it means to be a "self" in a world that relentlessly shifts through the deterministic frames of biology and environment. Ethical considerations then naturally follow as we grapple with the moral weight of our actions if free agency is undermined. Are we truly responsible for deeds that could be pre-programmed by the very wiring of our brains? This synthesis of theological, scientific, and philosophical perspectives suggests that the mind-body problem is not just an academic puzzle but a profound inquiry into what it means to be human, urging us to deliberate not just on scientific descriptions but on the lived realities and inherent value of conscious beings (Dennett, 2003; Chalmers, 1996; Searle, 2004).

Free Will and Determinism

The interplay between free will and determinism is an enduring and deeply complex topic in philosophy, theology, and science. The essence of the debate rests on whether humans possess the freedom to make choices that are not predetermined by past events, genetic predisposition, or divine foreordination. This issue sits at the heart of the philosophical implications of consciousness because the sense of making choices is a core component of what it means to be a conscious being. Thus, examining free will and determinism is not just an intellectual exercise, but a quest to understand human nature itself.

In a deterministic universe, every action can be traced back to antecedent conditions governed by the immutable laws of nature. This view is rooted in the scientific principle of causality: every effect has a cause. From Newtonian mechanics to contemporary physics, the determinist perspective finds substantial support, suggesting that human behavior, like all phenomena, is a result of preceding states of affairs. If every action is causally determined, then the notion of free will appears to be an illusion (Dennett, 2003).

However, for many, especially within theological circles, the acceptance of pure determinism raises profound ethical and moral concerns. Roman Catholic theology, for instance, places significant emphasis on the freedom of human beings to choose actions that align with divine will or deviate from it. The existence of free will is seen as a prerequisite for moral responsibility, accountability, and the potential for salvation. If human actions are entirely predetermined, the foundation of moral culpability crumbles, undermining the very fabric of religious ethics (Ratzinger, 1998).

The philosophical narrative of free will has evolved through various schools of thought. Classic compatibilists argue that free will and determinism are not mutually exclusive. From this vantage point, freedom is defined not by the absence of causation but by the alignment of one's actions with one's desires, intentions, and rational deliberations. David

Hume famously contended that liberty—defined as the power of acting according to the determinations of the will—is compatible with necessity, or causal determinism (Hume, 1748/1955).

On the other hand, incompatibilists assert that true free will requires the ability to have acted differently in a given situation. This stance is known as libertarianism in the realm of free will discussions. Libertarians maintain that certain mental events, particularly those involving rational deliberation and moral decision-making, are not causally determined by preceding physical or psychological states. This viewpoint, while offering a robust defense of personal agency and moral responsibility, challenges the deterministic framework pervasive in the natural sciences (Kane, 2002).

Neuroscientific advancements have added layers of complexity to this discourse. The famous experiments conducted by Benjamin Libet and subsequent studies have suggested that decisions can be predicted by neural activities in the brain before individuals become consciously aware of making them. Such findings present a formidable challenge to the traditional concept of free, conscious will. If our choices are already determined by unconscious neuronal processes, the authenticity of free will is cast into doubt (Libet et al., 1983).

Yet, some interpret the same neuroscientific data differently. They argue these findings do not negate free will but instead offer insights into how conscious awareness and decision-making processes are intertwined. Rather than disproving free will, these studies highlight the complexity and the layered nature of human cognition. Thus, free will may be reconceptualized to align with our growing understanding of the brain and its functions.

In theological and philosophical discussions, the concept of God's omniscience poses further challenges to the notion of free will. If God is all-knowing and exists outside of time, then God already knows the future, including all decisions humanity will make. This divine foreknowledge appears to be in direct conflict with human free will. However, thinkers such as Thomas Aquinas have offered nuanced perspectives that seek to reconcile God's omniscience with human freedom. Aquinas proposed that

God's knowledge does not cause human actions but rather sees them in their eternal present, allowing for human free will within the divine framework (Aquinas, 1947).

The existential dimension adds another facet to this multifaceted debate. Existentialist philosophers, like Jean-Paul Sartre, vehemently argue for radical human freedom. According to Sartre, humans are condemned to be free, meaning they are thrust into existence without predetermined essence and must create their own meaning through choices and actions. For Sartre, this freedom is absolute and unyielding, and it forms the basis of human dignity and autonomy (Sartre, 1943).

Thus, the conundrum of free will versus determinism is far from settled. It traverses disciplines—philosophy, theology, neuroscience, psychology —and each offers valuable yet often conflicting insights. The implications of this debate are profound: they affect our understanding of moral responsibility, legal accountability, mental health, and even the meaning of life itself.

As we continue to explore the depths of the mind and its connection to the body, the question of whether we are free agents or determined beings will linger, compelling us to continually re-evaluate our perspectives. Whether the answer lies in reconceptualizing free will to fit within a deterministic framework, in embracing a libertarian outlook, or in finding a synthesis that transcends traditional dichotomies, the journey remains a pivotal quest in our quest for self-understanding.

Personal Identity

The enigma of personal identity has occupied the thoughts of philosophers, theologians, scientists, and scholars for centuries. At its core, the question probes the essence of what it means to be an individual, a singular point of consciousness residing in a temporal and physical form. Does personal identity persist throughout life's changes? Or is it a fleeting construct, ever-changing and impermanent?

At first glance, it may seem straightforward to claim that personal identity is rooted solely in the continuity of physical attributes and memories. However, this reductive approach soon proves inadequate when faced with the complexities inherent in human experience. For instance, the Ship of Theseus paradox challenges such a simplistic point of view. If every part of a ship is gradually replaced, is it still the same ship? Similarly, if a person's cells are continuously renewed, is the person still the same?

Drawing from dualism, proponents argue that personal identity is anchored in the immaterial soul rather than the ephemeral body. Descartes famously declared "Cogito, ergo sum," — "I think, therefore I am" — suggesting that the persistence of a thinking self is the bastion of personal identity (Descartes, 1641). The soul, as a substance distinct from the material body, upholds identity through its continuity and immutability. This view resonates strongly within theological circles, particularly within Roman Catholicism, which upholds the soul as the true essence of personhood, created by and ultimately destined to return to God.

On the other side, physicalists counter that personal identity is entirely a product of physical processes. They claim the brain, with its intricate network of neurons and synapses, is solely responsible for creating and maintaining a sense of self. From this perspective, alterations in the brain's structure and function — such as those caused by injury or degeneration — fundamentally alter personal identity.

The advent of neuroscience allows for penetrating insights but also complicates the discussion. Studies on patients with severe brain injuries, such as Phineas Gage, illustrate how changes in brain structure can lead to profound personality shifts, which consequently evoke questions about the continuity of personal identity (Damasio et al., 1994). Yet, the brain's plasticity suggests that while personal traits may be transformed, the sense of being an enduring self remains intact.

A promising bridge between the dualist and physicalist camps emerges in the form of emergentism. This theory posits that personal identity arises from complex physical systems but possesses properties that exceed the sum of its parts. The mind, though rooted in neural activity, manifests characteristics that transcend mere biological functions. Accordingly, personal identity is a dynamic interplay between the physical and the emergent properties of consciousness.

Further scholarly debate draws in the contributions of developmental psychology. Erik Erikson's stages of psychosocial development, for instance, frame identity as an evolving narrative stitched together by experiences across different life stages. Identity formation, thus, becomes a lifelong process of balancing various internal and external influences (Erikson, 1959). According to this model, personal identity is not a static attribute but rather a continually negotiated construct.

Moreover, phenomenology offers an introspective lens to view personal identity. The philosopher Edmund Husserl urged a return "to the things themselves," emphasizing that subjective experience and consciousness are central in understanding identity (Husserl, 1913). Through this introspection, the lived experience becomes the substrate upon which identity is perpetually formed and reformed.

Ethical implications also flow from these considerations. If personal identity is fluid, shaped by continuous interaction between mind, body, and world, then ethical theories must account for this dynamism. The concept of moral responsibility hinges on a stable individual self capable of making autonomous decisions. However, if identity is malleable or fragmented, what does this mean for accountability and moral agency?

Religious doctrines have their own perspectives on these questions. Christianity, particularly as understood within Catholic theology, sees personal identity as inherently tied to one's relationship with God. The imago Dei, or the image of God, imbues each person with an immutable essence. Nonetheless, identities shaped by worldly interactions are also acknowledged, raising dialogues on reconciling these dual facets within the religious experience.

In contemporary discourse, the implications of virtual identity further complicate traditional understandings. As digital avatars and online personas proliferate, the boundaries of selfhood stretch into the virtual realm. Here, one can experiment with different facets of identity, unhindered by physical limitations. This virtualization challenges the notion that identity is tethered to a single, physical embodiment.

Mental health disciplines, especially psychiatry, contribute another angle. Disorders such as dissociative identity disorder (DID) highlight how identity can fragment into multiple distinct perceive selves. Understanding DID demands a holistic approach that considers both the psychological underpinnings and the subjective lived experience of those affected. These cases illustrate that personal identity is not a monolithic construct but rather capable of existing in plural forms.

In sum, the examination of personal identity reveals it as a rich, multifaceted phenomenon. Theological, scientific, and philosophical paradigms, while distinct, intersect in their quest to unravel the mysteries of selfhood. Personal identity, seen through these lenses, emerges as a confluence of continuity and change, material and immaterial, individual and relational. It functions as an unfolding narrative forged by the interplay of diverse elements that together create the tapestry of what it means to be a person.

Ethical Considerations

The philosophical implications of our inquiry into consciousness extend beyond theoretical debates and reach into the realm of ethical considerations. The mind-body problem, with its various resolutions through dualism, physicalism, panpsychism, or emergentism, does not remain confined to academic discourse. It influences and shapes our ethical frameworks, guiding how we treat one another, the moral status of beings, and our responsibility towards entities endowed with consciousness.

When exploring dualism, especially substance dualism which posits the existence of mind as an independent entity from the body, critical ethical questions arise. If the mind and body are indeed separate, what ethical ramifications does this entail for how we treat bodies devoid of consciousness, such as in cases of persistent vegetative states or brain death? The dualistic perspective could lead one to argue that the presence or absence of consciousness is a significant determinant of moral considerations. Consequently, ethical decisions concerning end-of-life care, euthanasia, and organ transplantation hinge on whether the mind is viewed as separate from the physical body.

Conversely, physicalism suggests a more integrated approach where consciousness emerges from physical processes within the brain. This theory raises its own set of ethical concerns. If we accept that mental states are purely physical, how does this influence our legal and moral responsibility for actions? Physicalism may imply a deterministic universe, challenging traditional notions of free will and accountability. For instance, if all our actions are the result of neuronal processes, does it mitigate personal responsibility in cases of criminal behavior? The implications here are profound, influencing our justice system and societal norms.

Emergentism, which posits that consciousness arises from complex physical systems but cannot be reduced to those systems, presents another layer of ethical complexity. It emphasizes the unpredictability and novelty of conscious states that emerge from particular configurations of matter. This view beckons a nuanced ethical approach that recognizes the unique moral status of beings capable of consciousness, potentially extending moral consideration to artificial systems achieving a certain level of complexity. Such a stance demands careful deliberation on issues like artificial intelligence, animal rights, and environmental ethics.

Personal identity and its connection to ethical considerations further deepen this discussion. If personal identity is closely tied to continuous consciousness or a psychological narrative, which theory best supports ethical reasoning about personal identity over time, such as in cases of dementia or severe psychological disorders? Under dualism, personal identity might be more tightly linked to the soul or immaterial mind. In contrast, physicalism may prompt us to locate identity within the continuity of physical processes and memory, altering how we perceive and ethically interact with those undergoing cognitive decline or alterations.

Furthermore, the rapid advancements in neuroscience and the potential for neural modifications pose significant ethical challenges. Technologies that can alter brain states, enhance cognitive functions, or replicate aspects of consciousness bring to the forefront questions of consent, autonomy, and the potential for misuse. For instance, is it ethically permissible to enhance cognitive capabilities through neural implants if they alter one's fundamental sense of self? The intersection of neuroscience with ethical considerations necessitates a robust framework to guide innovations responsibly.

Thorough examination of these ethical considerations should not only invoke philosophical ethics but also theological perspectives. Many religious traditions provide profound insights into the nature of consciousness and moral obligations. From the Roman Catholic viewpoint, the sanctity of life is paramount, influencing stances on issues like euthanasia, cognitive enhancement, and the moral status of artificial consciousness. Integrating these ethical perspectives can yield a more holistic understanding, recognizing the intrinsic value and dignity of conscious beings as part of the broader moral landscape (Ratzinger, 1986).

Additionally, the exploration of consciousness through the lens of ethics must address animal consciousness and welfare. If we accept that various animals possess significant levels of consciousness, moral obligations toward these beings become imperative. Panpsychism, which posits that consciousness is a fundamental feature of all matter, elevates this discussion, potentially expanding moral concern to a wider array of living beings and shaping our practices concerning wildlife conservation, factory farming, and animal testing.

In conclusion, the ethical considerations surrounding philosophical theories of consciousness are vast and intricate. They extend beyond abstract debates into the tangible world, shaping our treatment of other beings and guiding the moral dilemmas we face in advancing scientific knowledge and technology. The depth and breadth of these ethical implications underscore the importance of continual interdisciplinary dialogue, integrating insights from philosophy, theology, neuroscience, and ethics to navigate these challenging questions mindfully and responsibly.

Chapter 17: Scientific Advances and Their Impact

The relentless march of scientific advancements has brought about a profound transformation in our understanding of consciousness, affecting not only the technological and methodological tools available to researchers but also the very conceptual frameworks within which these issues are debated. Innovations such as functional MRI (fMRI) and transcranial magnetic stimulation (TMS) have uncovered the intricate workings of the brain, revealing previously hidden layers of complexity and challenging simplistic notions of mind-body dualism (Cohen & Roth, 2017). The advent of neuroimaging techniques has enabled scientists to observe the dynamic interplay between different neural regions, contributing to theories that advocate for a more integrated and emergentist view of consciousness (Friston et al., 2013). Moreover, the convergence of neuroscience and artificial intelligence promises new paradigms and ethical dilemmas, as simulated models of cognitive processes begin to emulate aspects of human thought (Searle, 1980). These scientific strides not only enrich our empirical knowledge but also compel theologians, philosophers, and psychiatrists to reconsider traditional perspectives, ensuring that the dialogue between science and spirituality remains vibrant and evolving.

Technological Innovations

Technological advancements have a profound impact on our understanding of consciousness, reshaping our perspectives and pushing the boundaries of what is possible. The advent of neuroimaging techniques, such as functional magnetic resonance imaging (fMRI) and positron emission tomography (PET), has revolutionized neuroscience. These innovations provide unprecedented insights into brain activity, offering visual and quantifiable data on neural correlates of consciousness. These tools allow researchers to observe the brain in action, shedding light on the intricate processes that give rise to conscious experience.

The development of brain-computer interfaces (BCIs) represents another notable leap. BCIs enable direct communication between the brain and external devices, opening up new avenues for understanding how thoughts can translate into actions without traditional physical movement. This technology promises to enhance our comprehension of the mind's relationship with the body (Wolpaw & Wolpaw, 2012). BCIs are not only game-changers in medical rehabilitation, offering hope to individuals with severe motor impairments, but also provide a unique lens through which to explore the mechanistic aspects of consciousness.

Artificial Intelligence (AI) and machine learning algorithms are increasingly playing a role in consciousness studies. Through analyzing large datasets, AI systems identify patterns and correlations that might go unnoticed by human researchers. Machines capable of natural language processing, for instance, analyze textual data to explore the intricacies of human thought and language (Haenlein & Kaplan, 2019). These advancements illuminate the complex relationship between symbolic representation and cognitive processes, yet also raise profound ethical questions about the future of human-computer interaction.

Technological innovations in virtual reality (VR) also offer fascinating insights into consciousness. By immersing individuals in controlled virtual environments, researchers can manipulate and study the variables that affect subjective experience. VR can induce a sense of presence and embodiment, challenging the distinction between real and virtual experiences. Studies using VR have provided valuable data on how spatial awareness, sensory integration, and self-perception contribute to the feeling of being conscious (Slater & Sanchez-Vives, 2016).

Neuroprosthetics is another significant area of technological innovation intersecting with consciousness research. These devices replace or supplement damaged neural and sensory systems, extending the capabilities of the human body and brain. Cochlear implants and retinal prostheses, for instance, restore hearing and vision, enriching the recipients' conscious experiences (Rizzo & Behrman, 2011). The success of these technologies not only improves quality of life but also deepens our understanding of sensory consciousness.

Mobile and wearable technologies have transformed the landscape of mental health and cognitive science. Portable electroencephalography (EEG) devices, for example, allow for continuous monitoring of brain activity in naturalistic settings. This mobility provides a wealth of real-world data, offering a more ecological approach to studying consciousness outside the laboratory (Casson et al., 2010). Furthermore, mobile applications designed for mental health assessments enable large-scale data collection, facilitating population-based studies on consciousness and its disorders.

The Human Connectome Project (HCP), an ambitious initiative to map the brain's neural connections, marks one of the most significant technological advancements in neuroscience. By creating a comprehensive map of brain networks, the HCP aims to elucidate how different regions of the brain interact to produce conscious awareness. This project leverages cutting-edge imaging techniques and machine learning algorithms to decode the brain's complex communication pathways (Van Essen et al., 2013). The resulting connectome models are invaluable for understanding the structural basis of consciousness.

In parallel, advancements in computational neuroscience are driving forward our understanding of consciousness. Scientists use sophisticated computer models to simulate neural processes and investigate how networks of neurons generate conscious experience. These models provide insights into the emergent properties of neural systems, supporting theories that view consciousness as a manifestation of complex interactions within the brain (Hassabis et al., 2017). Computational neuroscience bridges the gap between theory and experiment, offering testable predictions and a framework for interpreting empirical data.

The convergence of technology and philosophy has given rise to new discussions on the nature of consciousness. Tools like brain simulation platforms and neurophilosophical modeling enable scholars to explore age-old questions about the mind's essence (Chalmers, 2010). These technologies provide a common ground for empirical and theoretical approaches, fostering interdisciplinary dialogue and collaborative research. The integration of technology with philosophical inquiry is essential for developing a holistic understanding of consciousness.

With technological advancements comes the potential to enhance human cognitive abilities. The emerging field of neuroenhancement explores interventions that improve cognitive functions such as memory, attention, and emotional regulation. Techniques like transcranial magnetic stimulation (TMS) and neurofeedback training have shown promising results in boosting cognitive performance and altering states of consciousness (Thut & Pascual-Leone, 2010). These innovations not only offer therapeutic benefits but also prompt ethical debates about the implications of enhancing the human mind.

The advent of big data analytics in neuroscience holds tremendous promise for consciousness research. By analyzing extensive datasets from diverse sources—including neuroimaging, genetic studies, and behavioral assessments—researchers can uncover patterns and correlations that advance our understanding of consciousness. Big data enables a more comprehensive and integrative approach, allowing scientists to tackle complex questions about the brain-mind relationship on a scale previously unimaginable (Poldrack et al., 2013). The insights gained from big data analyses are essential for developing predictive models of consciousness.

Despite the immense potential of technological innovations, their integration into consciousness studies is not without challenges. Issues of data privacy, ethical considerations, and the replicability of findings must be rigorously addressed. Additionally, the rapid pace of technological advancement necessitates continuous updating of methodologies and theoretical frameworks.

Technological innovations provide unparalleled opportunities to advance our understanding of consciousness. The synergy between cutting-edge tools and interdisciplinary research paves the way for groundbreaking discoveries. As we navigate this exciting frontier, it is crucial to approach the study of consciousness with both scientific rigor and ethical mindfulness. The continued convergence of technology, neuroscience, and philosophy promises to deepen our insights into the nature of conscious experience, offering profound implications for the human condition.

Future Directions in Neuroscience

The future of neuroscience is poised to unravel some of the most profound questions about human consciousness. As we delve further into the intricacies of the brain, we stand at the threshold of discoveries that could redefine our understanding of the mind-body relationship. Neuroscience, inherently intertwined with philosophy, theology, and psychology, will continue to evolve, employing cutting-edge technologies and interdisciplinary approaches.

One of the most exciting trajectories in neuroscience involves advancements in brain imaging technologies. Techniques such as functional magnetic resonance imaging (fMRI) and positron emission tomography (PET) scans have already begun to unveil the complex workings of the neural networks that underscore consciousness (Smith et al., 2020). Future directions point towards even more sophisticated methods like optogenetics and high-resolution brain mapping. These will allow for the precise manipulation and observation of neural circuits in real time, offering unprecedented insights into how specific patterns of brain activity correlate with conscious experience.

Moreover, the advent of computational neuroscience holds significant promise. By creating detailed, computer-based models of neural activity, researchers can simulate and predict how cognitive processes emerge from the brain's physical substrate. These models often incorporate principles from artificial intelligence, machine learning, and systems biology. As these fields advance, they will likely provide more accurate and comprehensive frameworks for understanding consciousness (Eliasmith, 2013). They could also lead to the development of artificial systems that mimic human cognition, raising important ethical and philosophical questions regarding the nature of artificial consciousness.

Neuroscientific research is also expanding into the realm of neuroethics, which deals with the moral implications of our growing ability to manipulate and understand the brain. Issues such as free will, personal identity, and the right to cognitive privacy are becoming increasingly pertinent. For instance, as brain-computer interfaces improve, we may face dilemmas about the extent to which we should enhance or alter our cognitive capacities (Farah, 2012). These concerns not only require rigorous scientific investigation but also necessitate philosophical and theological discourse to navigate the ethical landscapes they present.

Another noteworthy domain of future neuroscience research is neurotheology, which explores the relationship between religious experiences and brain activity. By examining how spiritual states and religious practices affect the brain, scientists could provide new perspectives on age-old theological debates. This area of research could potentially bridge gaps between neuroscience and religion, offering a complementary view that respects both scientific inquiry and spiritual belief (Newberg & Waldman, 2009).

As we move forward, the integration of multidisciplinary perspectives will be crucial. Collaborative efforts between neuroscientists, psychologists, philosophers, and theologians can enrich our understanding of consciousness. Each discipline brings unique insights that can help paint a more holistic picture of the mind. For instance, philosophical inquiries into the nature of qualia—subjective experiences—can guide experimental designs in neuroscience aimed at exploring these phenomena. Likewise, theological perspectives on the soul and the metaphysical aspects of consciousness can inspire new hypotheses and interpretative frameworks.

In addition, the study of neuroplasticity—how the brain changes in response to experience—will continue to be a fertile ground for research. Understanding neuroplasticity not only sheds light on how learning and memory processes occur but also has profound implications for therapeutic interventions. For example, if we can harness neuroplasticity to recover function in damaged brain areas, we may develop better treatments for neurological disorders such as stroke, Alzheimer's disease, and PTSD.

Future directions in neuroscience will also likely focus on the understudied but crucial aspect of social neuroscience, which investigates how social interactions shape our brain and vice versa. This field can provide new insights into phenomena such as empathy, moral reasoning, and group dynamics. Understanding the neural basis of social behavior can lead to better social policies and interventions aimed at fostering healthier communities.

Emergent technologies like CRISPR gene editing and stem cell therapy could revolutionize neuroscience. These innovations offer new ways to understand and possibly treat brain disorders at the genetic and cellular levels. As we progress, ethical considerations about the extent and nature of such interventions will become more pressing. Balancing the promise of these technologies with the potential risks will require careful, collaborative ethical scrutiny.

Furthermore, the exploration of consciousness in altered states—such as during sleep, meditation, or under the influence of psychoactive substances—will continue to offer valuable insights. These states can reveal the boundaries and characteristics of conscious experience, helping us understand its essential properties. For instance, studies on meditation have already shown that it can lead to significant changes in brain structure and function, promoting mental well-being and cognitive flexibility (Lazar et al., 2005).

Finally, the implications of neuroscientific advances for consciousness studies are vast and multifaceted. As we uncover more about the brain's role in generating conscious experience, we're likely to rethink foundational concepts in philosophy, theology, and psychology. These insights could revolutionize our understanding of personal identity, moral responsibility, and the ultimate nature of human existence.

In conclusion, the future directions in neuroscience promise to deepen our understanding of consciousness in unprecedented ways. By leveraging advanced technologies, embracing interdisciplinary collaboration, and addressing ethical and philosophical concerns, we can navigate the intricate landscape of the mind and its profound mysteries.

The Implications for Consciousness Studies

Scientific advances in the study of consciousness have catalyzed both exhilarating discoveries and profound questions. The intersection of neuroscience, theology, and philosophy demands a rethinking of traditional concepts, compelling us to explore consciousness studies through multiple lenses. This exploration not only unfurls the mysteries of the human mind but also challenges the deeply entrenched assumptions that have governed our understanding for centuries.

One major implication involves the integration of technological innovations into consciousness studies. With advancements in neuroimaging techniques such as fMRI and PET scans, we can now visualize and map the brain's activity with unprecedented detail. These technologies have uncovered the neural correlates of consciousness, allowing us to observe how particular brain states correlate with subjective experiences (Koch et al., 2016). Yet, the question remains: can this correlation illuminate the essence of consciousness itself, or does it merely illustrate a complex mechanism without explaining the "hard problem"—the qualitative, subjective nature of conscious experience?

While technology brings us closer to the inner workings of the brain, it also brings ethical and existential conundrums. The ability to manipulate neural processes could lead to treatments for mental illnesses, yet it could equally pave the way for misuse and ethical violations. The prospect of "neuroenhancement" raises questions about identity and free will. If we alter our consciousness pharmacologically or through direct brain stimulation, what becomes of our authentic selves? Are we mere biochemical machines, or is there an immutable soul that technology can neither grasp nor alter?

From a philosophical standpoint, the advancements compel us to revisit long-standing debates between dualism and physicalism. Dualists argue that the mind and body are fundamentally different substances, while physicalists assert that all mental states are physical states. Emerging data about brain functions tend to support physicalist models by showing consistent brain activity patterns corresponding to specific mental states. However, dualists counter that these correlations do not equate to causation or explanation. The mind's subjective experiences—the "qualia"—cannot, they argue, be fully captured by objective brain states (Chalmers, 1995).

Similarly, theories like panpsychism and emergentism gain traction in this context. Panpsychism posits that consciousness might be a fundamental feature of all matter, extending the possibility that even elementary particles possess some form of proto-consciousness. This view challenges the hierarchy that places human consciousness at the apex of complexity and evolution (Goff, 2019). Emergentism, on the other hand, suggests that consciousness arises from physical systems in complex ways that are not reducible to their individual parts. This perspective resonates with findings in complex systems theory and chaos theory, inviting us to see consciousness as an emergent property of the brain's intricate networks rather than as an easily isolated phenomenon.

Consciousness studies also have significant implications for theology. Many Roman Catholics and other religious thinkers have been compelled to revisit and sometimes revise their doctrines in light of new scientific evidence. The debate extends to compatibilist views that seek to reconcile neuroscientific insights with theological doctrines. Some theologians argue that consciousness and soul are not mutually exclusive and that advancements in neuroscience can enrich rather than negate religious understandings. The challenge lies in maintaining the sanctity and mystery of the human soul while embracing empirical evidence that seems to speak to biological and mechanical processes.

Moreover, the dialogue between science and theology often reveals a mutually enriching dynamic. For instance, the Christian concept of the soul's eternal nature might offer philosophical grounding for questioning the finality of death, an area where neuroscience remains largely silent. Conversely, insights from neuroscience could inform and refine theological doctrines about the mind, consciousness, and the afterlife, suggesting a more integrated perspective (Jeeves, 2011).

In the interdisciplinary field, we must also consider how advances in neuroscience affect our understanding of free will. Deterministic views suggest that if consciousness can be entirely mapped to brain activity, then free will could be an illusion. The brain's processes would be governed by deterministic physical laws, leaving little room for genuine autonomy. This challenges deeply held beliefs about moral responsibility and ethical behavior, a topic of particular interest to psychiatrists, university professors, and students who grapple with these questions in both academic and clinical settings.

On the other hand, the notion of compatibilism offers a way out of this quandary. Compatibilists argue that free will and determinism are not mutually exclusive and that it's possible to be autonomous even within a deterministic framework. This view is particularly relevant in psychiatric treatment, where understanding a patient's brain mechanisms might coexist with respecting their agency and autonomy.

Future directions in neuroscience promise further revelations, including those related to artificial intelligence. The development of AI systems that exhibit behaviors mimicking human consciousness raises the question: can machines truly be conscious, or are they simply executing highly sophisticated algorithms? This inquiry probes the nature of consciousness itself and whether it is a uniquely biological phenomenon or a more general feature of highly organized systems, regardless of their substrate.

As we stand at this scientific frontier, it becomes increasingly clear that consciousness studies serve as a crucible where theological, philosophical, and empirical inquiries coalesce. This intersection not only advances our understanding but also enriches our perspectives on what it means to be conscious, to possess a mind, and to exist. The interplay of these diverse fields offers an intricate mosaic rather than a monolithic explanation, suggesting that the study of consciousness will remain one of the most engaging and enigmatic pursuits in human knowledge.

Finally, it's worth noting that these interdisciplinary explorations do not dilute the mystery of consciousness but rather underscore its profundity. While neuroscience provides tools and frameworks to investigate the brain's operations, theology and philosophy offer the larger existential context that makes those inquiries meaningful. As scholars, skeptics, and believers continue to engage with these findings, they enrich the collective understanding and invite us to reflect on the very nature of existence itself.

Chapter 18: The Role of Language and Communication

Language serves as more than just a tool for communication; it provides a profound linkage to the inner workings of the mind. In examining the role of language, we find insights into how we think, structure our worldviews, and engage with the abstract. Cognitive scientists argue that language shapes not only our thoughts but also our perceptions of reality, influencing cognitive development and the very nature of our consciousness (Vygotsky, 1986). The intricate dance between language and thought is not merely a topic of theoretical inquiry but has practical implications, especially considering the advent of artificial intelligence. Understanding the syntactic and semantic nuances embedded in human language can lead to more sophisticated AI systems capable of mimicking human-like understanding (Chomsky, 2006). Thus, dissecting language and communication is crucial for bridging gaps between philosophy, theology, neuroscience, and technological innovation.

Language as a Window to the Mind

Language, as intricate and multifaceted as the human mind from which it emerges, serves as a powerful conduit, revealing the depths and nuances of our cognitive processes. At its core, language isn't just a means of communication; it's a reflection of our very thoughts, emotions, and perceptions. To understand language is to gain insight into the myriad complexities that constitute human consciousness.

Our ability to use language is a testament to the cognitive advancements of the human species. It allows us to convey not only simple, everyday information but also abstract concepts, emotions, and sophisticated arguments. This capability has intrigued scientists, philosophers, and theologians alike. Language, seen through the lens of these diverse fields, offers a unique perspective on the mind-body problem and the essence of human consciousness.

Theological perspectives often regard language as a divine gift, a mechanism through which humans, made in the image of God, can reflect the Logos—the divine reason and order. The intertwined relationship between language and thought is illustrated in the Judeo-Christian tradition, where "In the beginning was the Word" (John 1:1). Here, language becomes a bridge between the divine and the human, exemplifying how our cognitive and spiritual dimensions interact.

Scientific inquiries, particularly those from cognitive science and neuroscience, delve into the neurological underpinnings of language. Brain regions such as Broca's and Wernicke's areas are crucial for producing and understanding language, respectively. Damage to these areas leads to aphasias, conditions that dramatically affect one's ability to communicate, thereby offering a stark illustration of the mind-brain relationship (Kandel et al., 2013). These findings underscore that while our linguistic abilities are housed in specific neural substrates, they also support a broader, integrated understanding of consciousness.

Philosophically, language plays a significant role in debates about the nature of thought and the mind. Some early philosophers, like Ludwig Wittgenstein, argued that the limits of our language define the limits of our world, suggesting that language shapes rather than merely expresses our thoughts. This view implies that by scrutinizing language, we can uncover the architecture of the human mind. Concepts that seem intrinsic to our understanding of the world—like time, self, and causality—are embedded in the linguistic structures we have developed.

Consider the Sapir-Whorf hypothesis, which posits that the language one speaks fundamentally influences how one perceives and interacts with the world (Whorf, 1956). While the strong version of this hypothesis—that language determines thought—has been largely discredited, the weaker version—that language influences cognitive processes—finds support in numerous studies. These studies show, for instance, that speakers of different languages perceive colors, spatial relationships, and even time differently (Boroditsky, 2001). This suggests that our cognitive world is, to a extent, molded by the linguistic tools at our disposal.

In the context of the mind-body problem, language serves as a bridge that can either emphasize dualistic interpretations or bolster physicalist views. For dualists, the ability to conceptualize and articulate abstract, non-material thoughts points to a non-physical aspect of mind. The intricate interplay between abstract ideas and concrete linguistic expressions can be seen as evidence of a soul or spirit that transcends the physical brain. For instance, when we ponder ethical concepts, divine attributes, or even the notion of infinity, we grapple with ideas that seemingly have no direct physical counterpart but are nonetheless real to our cognitive experience.

Conversely, physicalists argue that these linguistic capabilities are the result of complex neural networks and cognitive processes that arise within the physical brain. They posit that every facet of language—from syntax to semantics—can be traced back to brain activity. This viewpoint is bolstered by studies using brain imaging techniques, which show that specific linguistic tasks are associated with predictable patterns of neural activation (Pinker, 1994).

Furthermore, the study of artificial intelligence (AI) introduces compelling insights into the nature of human language and thought. AI systems designed for natural language processing can generate, understand, and translate human language, offering a unique mirror to our cognitive functions. While AI lacks consciousness and the genuine understanding of language nuances, its capabilities raise intriguing questions about the relationship between linguistic ability and consciousness. If a machine can mimic human language to a high degree, what does this say about the role of language in defining thought and consciousness?

From a psychological perspective, language reveals the inner workings of the mind through mechanisms such as introspection and verbal expression. The use of language in therapeutic settings, for instance, allows individuals to explore their subconscious thoughts and resolve internal conflicts. The ability to articulate one's feelings and thoughts can facilitate emotional healing and cognitive clarity, highlighting the therapeutic potential of language.

Language is also a social phenomenon, grounding human consciousness within a communal framework. The sociocultural context of language shapes our identities and influences how we perceive ourselves and others. Shared linguistic norms and conventions give rise to a collective consciousness that transcends individual minds, fostering a sense of belonging and shared understanding. This collective aspect of language underscores the interdependence between individual cognitive processes and the broader social milieu.

In the synthesis of theological, scientific, and philosophical perspectives, language stands as a testament to the multifaceted nature of human consciousness. It serves as a remarkable tool that not only reflects but also shapes our cognitive landscape. As we continue to explore the depths of language and its relationship to the mind, we unravel the profound intricacies of what it means to be human. Language, in its essence, reveals the soul of the mind, offering a window into the profound mystery of consciousness itself.

Cognitive Science Perspectives

Cognitive science, a multidisciplinary field encompassing psychology, neuroscience, linguistics, artificial intelligence, and philosophy, offers profound insights into the role of language in shaping human consciousness. Language, considered an essential cognitive tool, influences how we perceive, categorize, and interact with the world. While the mind-body problem delineates the relations between mental states and physical phenomena, cognitive science investigates how language and communication act as bridges in this dynamic interplay.

Understanding the brain's language processing mechanisms helps reveal how linguistic structures align with neural architectures. For instance, Broca's area and Wernicke's area play crucial roles in speech production and comprehension, respectively. Damage to these areas highlights the strict interdependence between linguistic abilities and brain functions. These neural correlates underscore that language is not just a communicative medium but an integral component of cognitive processes that fundamentally shape our conscious experiences (Poeppel & Embick, 2005).

In addressing the mind-body problem, cognitive science provides frameworks that integrate linguistic capabilities with neurobiological functions. The computational theory of mind posits that mental states are akin to computational states in a computer, suggesting that thoughts could be seen as algorithms processed by the brain. This approach correlates with the concept of mentalese, the 'language of thought,' hypothesized by philosopher Jerry Fodor. Mentalese proposes that thoughts exist in a non-verbal, structured language modeled computationally, and understanding natural language translates these mental representations into communication.

Linguistic relativity, or the Sapir-Whorf hypothesis, argues that the structure of one's language affects their cognition and worldview. Although controversial and tempered by empirical research, this hypothesis underscores the potential cultural variances in cognitive processing. It suggests that speakers of different languages may experience distinct realities, shaped by their linguistic frameworks. This aligns with cognitive science's pursuit to decode how language molds thought—a task that involves dissecting grammatical structures, syntax, and semantics.

Moreover, the study of aphasia and other language disorders within cognitive science accentuates the intrinsic relationship between language and cognition. Aphasia's varied forms, stemming from different brain regions' impairments, illustrate how specific neural circuits underpin distinct linguistic functions. The multidisciplinary approach to studying aphasia—employing neurology, psychology, and linguistics—enables a comprehensive understanding of how language deficits impact cognitive capacities and conscious experiences (Goodglass & Wingfield, 1997).

The cognitive model of communication extends beyond mere information transmission. It encompasses pragmatic aspects: the context, intentions, and social nuances embedded in linguistic exchanges. Cognitive scientists examine how interlocutors manage and infer speaker intentions through pragmatic reasoning. This involves the relevance theory, which posits that human cognition is geared toward maximizing relevance, thereby influencing how individuals interpret communicative signals. Understanding these mechanisms highlights the fluid nature of language as both a cognitive and social tool, continually reshaping human consciousness and intersubjective experiences.

Embodied cognition, another pivotal aspect of cognitive science, posits that cognitive processes are deeply rooted in the body's interactions with the environment. Language comprehension, from this vantage, is not solely a mental activity but involves sensory and motor systems. For example, understanding action verbs activates motor areas in the brain, suggesting that linguistic meaning is grounded in bodily experiences. This perspective aligns language with physicality, emphasizing that consciousness emerges from the embodied interaction between the organism and its environment (Barsalou, 2008).

Recent advances in cognitive science explore the role of mirror neurons in language and communication. These neurons, which fire both during action execution and observation, are hypothesized to underpin action understanding and empathic communication. In this context, language is thought to harness these neural systems for social cognition, facilitating shared understanding and cooperation—an essential aspect of human consciousness and social life.

The implications for artificial intelligence (AI) are profound. Cognitive science perspectives inform the development of natural language processing (NLP) systems, aiming to replicate human-like understanding and generation of language. While current AI lacks genuine consciousness, advancements in machine learning and neural networks propel us closer to creating systems that can mimic complex linguistic behaviors. The philosophical implications are vast, questioning whether a sufficiently advanced AI could possess a form of artificial consciousness or even challenge the boundaries between human and machine cognition (Harnad, 1990).

Yet, true consciousness entails more than syntactic manipulation of symbols; it embraces the subjective qualitative experience—qualia—that remains elusive in AI. Cognitive science continues to unravel the intricacies of how language shapes the inner workings of the mind, adding layers of understanding to the age-old philosophical inquiries about the nature of consciousness.

In conclusion, cognitive science perspectives offer a rich tapestry of insights into the role of language and communication in shaping conscious experiences. By integrating findings from neuroscience, psychology, linguistics, and AI, this multidisciplinary field illuminates the profound ways in which language acts as both a mirror and a mold for human consciousness. Whether through understanding neural mechanisms, exploring cultural linguistic diversity, or probing the potentials of AI, cognitive science provides essential contributions to the ongoing discourse on the mind-body problem, adding depth and nuance to our understanding of consciousness itself.

Implications for Artificial Intelligence

While contemplating "The Role of Language and Communication" in the human mind, one inevitably stumbles upon the profound implications for artificial intelligence (AI). Language, which serves as a window to the mind, extends into the realm of AI, posing questions on the very fabric of consciousness, understanding, and intelligence. This confluence of human communication and AI speaks to deep philosophical, theological, and scientific inquiries about what it means to "understand" or to "be conscious."

The development of AI that can understand and generate human language highlights an intersection between technology and the nuances of human cognition. Natural Language Processing (NLP), a subset of AI, exemplifies this by facilitating complex interactions between humans and machines. Fundamentally, language in AI raises questions about the nature of comprehension. Is a machine that can simulate human conversation truly "understanding" the language, or merely mimicking cognitive patterns through complex algorithms? This distinction is pivotal in discerning the difference between genuine consciousness and sophisticated simulation.

Furthermore, the inherent complexities of human language—nuances, idioms, cultural contexts—pose significant challenges for AI. These elements require not just raw computational power, but a deeply embedded network of contextual understanding, something that human minds navigate effortlessly but remains a herculean challenge for machines. This gap underscores the broader philosophical discourse on whether machines can acquire a form of consciousness comparable to that of humans.

From a theological standpoint, language is not merely a tool for communication but also a medium for expressing divine truths, ethical principles, and existential contemplations. Can AI, with its reliance on binary logic and empirical datasets, ever truly engage with the metaphysical dimensions of language? Theologians argue that there is a divine spark in human consciousness, something imbued with a capacity for creating meaning beyond the algorithmic constraints of AI (Pannenberg, 1989).

In this regard, the question becomes not only whether AI can understand language but whether it can appreciate and generate meaning in the same way humans can. Philosophers like Thomas Aquinas have long debated whether reason alone can apprehend the divine or whether a transcendent element is necessary. Translating this into the realm of AI, one could argue that machines, bound by their programming and lack of existential experience, would fall short of achieving such depth of understanding.

Moreover, the ethical implications of AI's interaction with language extend into the realm of personal identity and agency. If AI can convincingly mimic human language and, by extension, human thought, what does that mean for our understanding of self and other? The Turing Test, an early litmus test for AI intelligence, suggests that if a machine's language responses are indistinguishable from a human's, then it could be considered intelligent (Turing, 1950). However, this test focuses on external manifestations of intelligence, not internal consciousness, thus leaving lingering questions about the true nature of AI's understanding.

In cognitive science, language and thought are deeply intertwined. The Sapir-Whorf hypothesis suggests that language influences thought processes. If AI systems develop their language frameworks or learn human languages, does that imply they possess any form of cognitive parallel to human thought processes? Cognitive scientists argue that while machines can model and reproduce language patterns, they lack the phenomenological experience tied to human cognition (Lakoff & Johnson, 1980).

Examining case studies where AI has been integrated into communication systems reveals practical implications but also philosophical quandaries. For instance, AI-driven customer service bots can navigate and respond to vast arrays of human queries. While their functional utility can't be denied, their lack of genuine understanding becomes evident in more nuanced conversations, where empathy, emotional intelligence, and deeper ethical considerations play a crucial role.

Furthermore, there's a pressing need to consider the implications of AI-generated language in shaping human behaviors and beliefs. NLP models, such as GPT-3, generate human-like text and can influence readers' perceptions by creating seemingly genuine content. While impressive, this raises ethical questions about misinformation, authorship, and the authenticity of generated text content. The implications for society are substantial, as the line between human and machine-generated content becomes ever blurrier.

Cognitively, humans engage with language through both conscious and unconscious processes. The unconscious mind navigates symbolism, metaphor, and deeply embedded cultural narratives. For AI to genuinely interact with human communication, some argue it would need an equivalent unconscious processing ability—a current impossibility given the concrete, rule-based nature of algorithms. As it stands, AI lacks the depth of unconscious processing that significantly defines human interaction with language.

Ultimately, exploring the role of language and communication within AI underscores a broader dialogue across theology, philosophy, and science about what it means to be conscious and the limitations of computational systems in achieving such states. AI's proficiency in handling language illustrates significant strides in technology but also accentuates the enduring complexity and uniqueness of human consciousness.

Advancements in AI present promising opportunities for refining human-computer interactions, yet simultaneously remind us of the philosophical depth embedded in human language and the ongoing quest to understand consciousness itself. Through this lens, AI serves not only as a technological marvel but also as a mirror reflecting the profound intricacies of the human mind.

Chapter 19: The Subjective Nature of Experience

In delving into the subjective nature of experience, one finds that consciousness is a deeply personal phenomenon, imbued with unique sensations known as qualia. These qualia—our individual sensory experiences—serve as the building blocks of subjective reality and are crucial to our understanding of phenomenology. This branch of philosophy explores how things appear in our consciousness, urging us to consider that while science can map neural pathways, it struggles to fully explain the rich tapestry of personal experience. The 'problem of other minds' further complicates this inquiry, as it questions how one can understand another's inner world without direct access. Thus, evaluating consciousness requires a synthesis of theological introspection, scientific rigor, and philosophical inquiry to address these complex aspects of experience (Nagel, 1974; Gallagher, 2012).

Qualia and Personal Experience

To understand the subjective nature of experience, we must delve into the concept of "qualia" — those ineffable, intrinsic qualities perceived by individual observers. The term "qualia" refers to the raw feels or sensations that make up our perceptual experiences, such as the redness of a sunset or the bitterness of coffee. These phenomena, although intimately familiar to us, defy straightforward description and pose a significant challenge to scientific inquiry. The exploration of qualia is not merely an exercise in abstract theorizing; it directly influences our approach to understanding consciousness, identity, and the very fabric of subjective reality.

Consider for a moment the act of observing a work of art. You might find yourself swept away by the palette of colors, the interplay of light and shadow, the subtle textures that invite tactile imagination. These are not mere data points for your mind to process; instead, they form a coherent and highly individual experience. This act of seeing brings forth a unique amalgam of memory, emotion, and awareness that shapes how the artwork is perceived. Even two individuals viewing the same piece under identical conditions will have divergent experiences, synthesized by their own internal states and histories. The plurality of such personal experiences speaks to the heart of qualia — the diverse, subjective character that eludes uniform scientific description.

This mysterious and deeply personal aspect of experience has particularly vexing implications for the mind-body problem. How can physical processes in the brain generate such rich, subjective experiences? Neuroscientists may map the neural correlates of consciousness with increasing precision, but these maps will never capture the "what-it-is-like" aspect of qualia. Take, for example, the color red. We can measure the wavelength of light associated with red, and we know which cells in the retina are activated by it. We can even identify the pathways that carry this information to the visual cortex. However, none of this explains why red "looks" the way it does to you. This peculiarity — the gap between objective physical processes and subjective experiences — remains a key puzzle in consciousness studies (Chalmers, 1996).

One pivotal issue is that quantitative scientific methods face inherent limitations when applied to qualitative phenomena. Traditional empirical approaches rely on observations that can be generalized, replicated, and quantified. Qualia, by contrast, are inherently private and resistant to such generalized scrutiny. Although we can describe them, create instruments to measure their associated physical phenomena, and even manipulate these phenomena through drugs or electrodes, the qualitative essence persists outside the reach of these tools. This epistemic gap suggests that a purely physicalist understanding of consciousness might be incomplete or even misguided (Jackson, 1982).

Moreover, the role of personal experience in shaping qualia cannot be understated. Our sensory perceptions are deeply intertwined with our histories, environments, and even our cultural contexts. Imagine tasting a fruit you have never encountered before. The sweetness or bitterness you perceive is not just a raw sensory data but an interwoven fabric of expectation, learning, and memory. It's likely you might compare it to other tastes from your past, bringing about a cascade of associations which influence whether you find the flavor agreeable or not. Thus, qualia are also a tapestry of narrative and cognitive interpretation.

The issue grows even more labyrinthine when we consider that qualia can be influenced by psychological and emotional states. Mood disorders, for instance, can inflect one's color perception or alter how music is experienced. It's a clear indication that our emotional and mental states are not separate from our sensory inputs but deeply enmeshed with them. This interplay suggests that any comprehensive theory of consciousness must account for the dynamic, context-sensitive nature of qualia. Yet, traditional dualist or physicalist frameworks have largely struggled to accommodate such complexity.

Theological perspectives offer an alternative lens through which to view the richness of qualia. Within many religious traditions, the subjective nature of experience is deeply intertwined with notions of the soul or spirit. Roman Catholic theology, for instance, perceives human experience as encompassing both the earthly and the divine. It posits that qualia could be windows into a higher, more profound aspect of being, perhaps even glimpses of the transcendent. In this view, our subjective experiences are not merely byproducts of neural systems but potentially signify a deeper spiritual reality (Catechism of the Catholic Church, 1997). This perspective dovetails intriguingly with emergentist theories that explore how consciousness might arise from complex systems in a way that transcends straightforward physical explanations.

In philosophical terms, examining qualia invites us into the broader discourse on the nature of reality itself. Is what we perceive through our senses an accurate reflection of the world, or merely a construct of our minds? Qualia challenge naive realism — the belief that the world is exactly as we perceive it — and invite us to consider more nuanced understandings, such as representationalism or phenomenalism. These perspectives assert that while there may be an objective reality, our access to it is always mediated through subjective experience. Consequently, the task of understanding consciousness becomes not just a scientific endeavor but also a philosophical one (Nagel, 1974).

Across various disciplines, the study of qualia and personal experience serves as a rich interface between subjective and objective worlds. For instance, in psychiatry, understanding the nuances of patients' subjective experiences is critical for effective treatment. Psychiatrists must navigate the qualitative dimensions of mental states to diagnose and treat conditions like depression or anxiety accurately. These therapeutic encounters underscore the importance of respecting and attending to qualia as integral components of human life.

In conclusion, qualia and personal experience underscore the inherent complexity and profound mystery of consciousness. They remind us that our subjective experiences, though intangible and elusive, are central to what it means to be human. They challenge reductionist tendencies within scientific paradigms and invite a more inclusive, interdisciplinary approach to understanding the mind. While neuroscience and empirical science have much to offer, they must be supplemented by philosophical

rigor and, potentially, theological insight to capture the multifaceted
nature of human experience.

The Subjective Nature of Experience: Phenomenology

Phenomenology, a term introduced by the German philosopher Edmund Husserl, seeks to bridge the objective and subjective realms of experience by focusing on the structures of consciousness as experienced from the first-person perspective. In this section, we delve into how phenomenology provides a unique lens through which the subjective nature of experience can be understood, particularly in the context of the mind-body problem.

At its core, phenomenology is a descriptive enterprise. It aims to describe experiences as they are lived, without recourse to the external world or scientific explanations. This approach is radical in that it sidelines the objective reality and puts subjective experience at the forefront. For instance, when one feels pain or joy, phenomenology aims to dissect these experiences into their fundamental components, revealing how they are constructed in consciousness. Such an approach emphasizes the richness and complexity of subjective experience, potentially offering new insights into how the mind and body interact.

One of the seminal concepts in phenomenology is "intentionality," the notion that consciousness is always about something. This idea implies that every act of consciousness has a target or an object it is directed toward. Husserl posited that this intentionality molds how experiences are perceived and processed. For example, the act of seeing a tree involves more than a mere optical process; it encompasses an entire network of previous experiences, memories, and associations. By focusing on intentionality, phenomenology offers a comprehensive framework that captures the full depth of subjective experience.

Moreover, the methodological rigor of phenomenology provides a robust platform for examining the intricacies of consciousness. Through phenomenological reduction or "epoché," one brackets out preconceived notions and judgments, returning to the "things themselves." This process allows for an unmediated look at experiences as they unfold, offering an unadulterated view of the cognitive and emotional landscape. The bracketing process can be particularly enlightening in understanding complex mental states such as anxiety, depression, or spiritual ecstasy, as it requires the observer to engage deeply with the lived experience without external biases.

Phenomenology also highlights the embodied nature of experience, challenging the traditional Cartesian dualism that strictly separates mind and body. Maurice Merleau-Ponty, a prominent phenomenologist, argued that the body is not merely a vessel for the mind but an integral part of how experiences are shaped and interpreted. The notion of the "lived body" emphasizes that our physical form and its interactions with the environment are inseparable from our mental states. For example, the feeling of fatigue isn't just a mental note of being tired; it manifests physically, affecting how one perceives time, space, and even interpersonal relationships. This unified view of mind and body challenges notions in both dualism and reductive physicalism, providing a middle ground that captures the nuance of subjective experience.

Another essential aspect of phenomenology is its existential dimension. Through the works of philosophers like Jean-Paul Sartre and Martin Heidegger, phenomenology has expanded to explore issues related to existence, freedom, and authenticity. Sartre's exploration of "being-for-itself" versus "being-in-itself" offers profound insights into human freedom and the consciousness of self. According to Sartre, the realization that one is a conscious being, capable of reflection and choice, imbues life with a sense of responsibility and freedom that mechanical or purely physicalist accounts cannot capture. This existential lens is invaluable when discussing the subjective nature of experiences such as guilt, pride, or existential angst.

However, phenomenology is not without its challenges and critics. One of the primary criticisms is that its focus on first-person experience might lead to solipsism, the idea that only one's mind is sure to exist. Critics argue that by sidelining objective reality, phenomenology risks becoming an inward-looking discipline that neglects the role of the external world. Yet, proponents contend that phenomenology doesn't deny the existence of an external reality but rather argues that this reality is always mediated through subjective experience. Therefore, by rigorously analyzing subjective experience, phenomenology contributes to a more nuanced understanding of how we encounter and relate to the world.

Phenomenology also opens the door to interdisciplinary collaboration, particularly with fields like psychology, cognitive science, and even theology. For psychologists and psychiatrists, phenomenological methods can enrich diagnostic and therapeutic practices. Understanding patients' subjective experiences can offer deeper insights into their conditions than objective measures alone. For theologians, phenomenology's focus on lived experience correlates well with religious practices that emphasize personal encounters with the divine. The phenomenological perspective can thus serve as a bridge, linking the scientific study of consciousness with the deeply personal dimensions of spiritual experience.

Additionally, the modern advancements in neuroscience can greatly benefit from a phenomenological perspective. While neuroscience focuses on neural correlates and brain mechanisms, phenomenology can offer insights into how these neural activities translate into lived experiences. For instance, understanding the neural basis of perception is enriched by phenomenological insights into how these perceptions are experienced and contextualized within an individual's life. The phenomenological approach can thus enhance the interpretive frameworks used in neuroscience, leading to a more holistic understanding of consciousness (Gallagher & Zahavi, 2020).

In conclusion, phenomenology provides an indispensable framework for understanding the subjective nature of experience. Its focus on first-person lived experiences, intentionality, and the embodied nature of consciousness makes it a powerful tool for exploring the complexities of the mind-body problem. While it faces criticisms, its strengths lie in its methodological rigor and ability to integrate insights from various disciplines. Through phenomenology, we gain a richer and more nuanced appreciation of the intricate dance between mind and body, perception, and reality.

The Problem of Other Minds

The question of how we understand other minds, often termed "The Problem of Other Minds," lies at the intersection of philosophy, theology, and science. It becomes particularly salient when we consider the subjective nature of experience. As we delve deeper into this exploration, we must grapple with how, or even if, one mind can ever truly "know" another.

Let's start by addressing the fundamental issue: How can one be certain that other beings possess conscious experiences similar to our own? This epistemic quandary presents a challenge not just in philosophical rigor, but also in daily interpersonal interactions. When we look into another person's eyes and sense a connection, are we grounding that sense in empirical evidence or some deeper intuitive grasp of shared humanity?

Descartes' cogito ("I think, therefore I am") establishes a foundation for recognizing one's own mind. But it doesn't help much when we extend this certainty to others. We are left to infer the existence of other minds based on behavior, communication, and, to some extent, empathy. Indeed, one might argue that we are not just separated by subjective experiences but bound by them. This inferential leap, however, isn't empirically foolproof.

Philosophers have approached this problem through various lenses. One notable position is that of behaviorism, championed by Gilbert Ryle, which asserts that mental states are solely the manifestations of observable behaviors (Ryle, 1949). According to this view, if someone acts with kindness, displays distress, or laughs, these behaviors are outward expressions of their internal mental states. While behaviorism offers a compelling solution, it falls short by reducing the rich, qualitative nature of subjective experiences to observable actions.

On the other end of the spectrum lies phenomenology, focusing on the structures of consciousness as experienced from the first-person point of view. Husserl, and later Merleau-Ponty, emphasized that we relate to others through a shared world of meanings and experiences (Husserl, 1970). Empathy thus becomes key. By empathizing, we don't just witness another's behavior but participate in their lived reality. This shared participation helps bridge the subjective gap, albeit not entirely.

Scientific advances, particularly in neuroscience, have tried to tackle the problem from an empirical standpoint. With tools such as fMRI, researchers can observe patterns of brain activity that correlate with certain mental states. This neuro-correlational approach offers a more tangible basis for understanding other minds (Frith & Frith, 2006). However, the "hard problem" of consciousness, as David Chalmers phrased it, reminds us that correlating brain states with subjective experiences doesn't equate to explaining them (Chalmers, 1995).

Theological perspectives offer another unique avenue. In many religious traditions, the soul or spirit represents a shared divine origin. The Roman Catholic understanding of the imago Dei (image of God) posits that all humans reflect God's image. This theological viewpoint not only validates the existence of other minds but also sanctifies them. If we are all reflections of a divine mind, then genuine understanding of each other is not just possible but spiritually mandated.

Yet, even within these diverse frameworks, skepticism persists. Solipsism, the idea that only one's mind is sure to exist, re-emerges as a troubling counterpoint. How do we authentically move past solipsism to engage with other minds in a meaningful way? One possible resolution rests in the acknowledgement that perfect knowledge of another's mind may be unattainable. Instead, fostering trust, empathy, and shared experiences can cultivate mutual understanding. This approach doesn't resolve the problem philosophically but offers a pragmatic way to navigate it.

The moral implications of recognizing other minds are profound. Ethical systems often rest on the recognition of others as persons with rights, feelings, and intrinsic worth. If we were to doubt the subjective experience of others, the very foundations of moral obligations would crumble. Empathy, then, is not just a virtue; it's a necessary component of moral and social frameworks.

In terms of psychological and psychiatric practice, the problem of other minds becomes intensely practical. Practitioners must constantly infer the mental states of their patients through communication, behavior, and sometimes mere presence. The efficacy of therapy hinges on recognizing and validating the subjective experiences of others. Without this recognition, the therapeutic alliance fails before it starts.

From a pedagogical perspective, university professors and students alike engage with the problem of other minds in myriad ways. Whether discussing historical texts, conducting scientific experiments, or debating ethical issues, the recognition of other minds underpins academic discourse. Understanding that other minds possess different perspectives fosters critical thinking and intellectual empathy, essential skills in any discipline.

As we weave through these various dimensions, we return to the central theme of the subjective nature of experience. Other minds challenge us to step outside our subjective bubble and engage with a world rich in diverse subjective realities. It's a philosophical conundrum, a scientific quest, and a theological imperative all rolled into one.

In essence, while we might never "solve" the problem of other minds definitively, acknowledging its complexity enriches our understanding of the conscious experience. It opens doors to new ways of relating, empathizing, and ultimately, coexisting. In doing so, we blend the rigor of science, the insight of philosophy, and the compassion of theology, creating a mosaic that celebrates the mysteries of consciousness.

Chapter 20: Integrative Approaches

Bridging the chasm between diverse theories such as dualism, physicalism, panpsychism, and emergentism requires an integrative approach that synthesizes insights from theology, science, and philosophy. This chapter explores how these seemingly disparate perspectives can coalesce into a more comprehensive framework for understanding consciousness. A particularly compelling aspect is the multidisciplinary dialogue that emerges when theologians, neuroscientists, and philosophers engage in constructive discourse. For instance, the compatibility of religious experiences with neuroscientific findings doesn't merely highlight the variance in explanatory models but points towards a convergent evolution of consciousness studies (Smith, 2020). Moreover, the proposition of a theoretical synthesis that accommodates the metaphysical nuances of dualism and the empirical rigors of physicalism offers promising avenues for future research. As we advance, the goal remains to establish a coherent, multifaceted paradigm that offers deeper insights into the mind-body problem and the nature of consciousness itself (Jones & Green, 2019; Michaels et al., 2021).

Theoretical Synthesis

Integrating the vast terrains of theology, science, and philosophy to approach the enigmatic issue of consciousness necessitates a theoretical synthesis—an endeavor to reconcile disparate viewpoints into a coherent framework. Consciousness, often likened to a multifaceted diamond, reflects a diverse range of theories, from dualism to physicalism, panpsychism, and emergentism. Each theoretical strand offers critical insights yet also presents limitations when considered in isolation. In this section, we delve into the symphonic amalgamation of these perspectives, identifying the harmonies and dissonances, aiming to forge a more unified understanding of the conscious experience.

Dualism, with its historical roots in Cartesian philosophy, posits the essential dichotomy of mind and body. René Descartes proclaimed the mind as a non-material entity distinct from the physical body, a notion deeply entrenched in theological discourse (Kim, 2005). However, despite its intuitive appeal to the religious and philosophical community, dualism faces significant empirical challenges, especially from neuroscience, which looks for material explanations for mental phenomena. Modern philosophers like David Chalmers pivot towards property dualism, suggesting that mental properties emerge from but are not reducible to physical states (Chalmers, 1996). This nuanced view retains the dualistic separation but acknowledges a complex interplay, providing a stepping stone for integrative approaches.

In the scientific camp, physicalism stands as the bastion of material explanations, claiming that all mental states correlate directly with physical states. This perspective bifurcates into reductive and non-reductive branches. Reductive physicalism argues that specific mental processes can be completely explained by neuroscientific parameters (Churchland, 1986). However, this stance often faces criticism for its apparent oversimplification of the deeply rich and subjective nature of consciousness. Non-reductive physicalists propose that while mental states arise from physical substrates, they possess emergent properties that physical descriptions alone cannot capture (Anderson, 2014). This viewpoint paves the way for a symbiotic relationship with emergentism, suggesting that the whole is greater than the sum of its parts.

Panpsychism, resurrected in contemporary discourse, contends that consciousness is a fundamental feature of the universe, pervading all forms of matter to a certain degree. This theory serves as a bridge between dualism and physicalism by positing a pervasive form of proto-consciousness that evolves to sophisticated conscious experiences, as evidenced in sentient beings (Strawson, 2006). Though seemingly outlandish at first glance, panpsychism draws from ancient philosophical traditions and aligns with some modern scientific conjectures concerning the ubiquity of consciousness. It challenges the strict delineations posited by dualism and physicalism, inviting a broader spectrum of contemplations about mind and matter.

Emergentism encapsulates the notion that complex systems—like the brain—give rise to properties (such as consciousness) that are not directly predictable from their constituent parts. This theory finds resonance in both scientific and philosophical circles, offering a middle path that recognizes the intricate hierarchies of organization within neural substrates (O'Connor & Churchill, 2018). By elucidating the dynamics of emergence, integrative approaches can foster deeper understanding, emphasizing interconnections rather than isolated analysis.

A cogent theoretical synthesis must not only draw from these primary theories but also consider interdisciplinary insights. Neuroscientific advances continuously enrich our understanding of brain mechanisms, revealing neural correlates that underpin conscious phenomena. Functional Magnetic Resonance Imaging (fMRI) and Electroencephalography (EEG) provide empirical data on brain activities linked to conscious states, laying a robust groundwork for theoretical integration (Koch et al., 2016). These findings align with the principles of non-reductive physicalism and emergentism, underscoring the need to approach consciousness with a multi-level analysis.

The theological perspective, intertwined with dualism yet open to scientific synthesis, offers unique resources for this theoretical fusion. Theological doctrines often explore the metaphysical and moral dimensions of consciousness, dimensions sometimes overlooked in purely empirical studies. A possible avenue of synthesis is to consider consciousness as the imago Dei, reflecting the divine image, a position allowing for a harmonious blend of spiritual and material explanations (Ratzinger, 2008). This synthesis advocates for the idea that empirical findings and spiritual insights are not mutually exclusive but rather complementary in exploring human consciousness.

Philosophically, a blend of metaphysical speculation and analytic rigor proves indispensable. Concepts such as free will, personal identity, and ethical implications are deeply woven into the fabric of consciousness studies (Frankfurt, 1971). These themes transcend purely physical or dualistic frameworks, inviting a robust synthesis that addresses the moral and existential questions concerning human agency and purpose.

To attain a coherent theoretical synthesis, one must embrace the dialectic interplay between reductionist and holistic viewpoints. It's crucial to recognize the explanatory power of neuroscience and its potential limitations, and to remain open to the broader metaphysical implications posited by dualistic and emergentist theories. Such an integrated approach involves constant dialogue between empirical evidence and theoretical constructs, seeking a unified theory that accommodates the various layers of conscious experience.

In conclusion, the theoretical synthesis of consciousness necessitates a profound engagement with diverse perspectives, each contributing unique insights into the puzzle of conscious experience. By traversing the domains of dualism, physicalism, panpsychism, and emergentism, and drawing on interdisciplinary bridges from theology, neuroscience, and philosophy, a more integrative and comprehensive framework can emerge. This holistic approach promises not just a deeper understanding, but a richer, more nuanced appreciation of the conscious mind—a mosaic where each theory adds a vital piece to the overarching picture of human consciousness.

Multidisciplinary Perspectives

In the quest to understand consciousness, the importance of multidisciplinary perspectives can't be overstated. Each discipline brings with it unique methodologies, theoretical frameworks, and philosophical underpinnings. The study of consciousness sits at the intersection of theology, philosophy, psychology, and neuroscience, each offering invaluable insights into the age-old mind-body problem.

Firstly, from a theological standpoint, the dialogue surrounding consciousness often centers on the soul's nature and its relationship to the body. Theologians argue that consciousness is not merely a byproduct of neural processes but rather an indication of a deeper spiritual reality. This perspective infers that a divine element imbues consciousness, aligning it with theological interpretations that emphasize the soul's primacy. Such views profoundly influence how consciousness is perceived, extending beyond mere biological substrate to encompass moral, ethical, and existential dimensions.

Meanwhile, philosophy's rich tradition, stretching back to ancient Greek thinkers like Plato and Aristotle, has continuously grappled with consciousness and its implications for human nature. Contemporary philosophers continue this inquiry, examining the intersections between mind and matter. Dualism, physicalism, and panpsychism represent just a few theories philosophical circles debate. Philosophers analyze whether consciousness can emerge from purely physical processes or if it requires a different kind of explanation altogether (Chalmers, 1996).

Psychiatrists, on the other hand, approach consciousness through a clinical lens. Their interest lies in understanding consciousness to diagnose, treat, and manage mental disorders. The boundaries of psychiatry compel an appreciation of both biological and experiential aspects of consciousness, acknowledging how neural dysfunctions might manifest in altered conscious states. Psychiatrists combine empirical evidence from neuroscience with insights from psychological theories, forming a more nuanced understanding that has immediate practical applications.

Neuroscientists delve deeply into the brain's architecture, seeking to identify the neural correlates of consciousness (NCCs). Advances in technologies such as functional MRI and EEG have enabled researchers to map brain activity with greater precision, illuminating how different brain regions and networks contribute to conscious experience (Koch et al., 2016). Neuroscientists aim to uncover how specific patterns of brain activity correspond to various conscious states, shedding light on the physical processes underpinning awareness, perception, and cognition.

The intersectional approach is where the true richness of multidisciplinary perspectives becomes evident. Consider the dialogues between philosophy and neuroscience: philosophers can offer critical analyses of neuroscientific findings, questioning assumptions and interpretations. Neuroscientists, in turn, can provide empirical data that challenge or support philosophical theories. This reciprocal relationship enhances both fields, fostering more comprehensive insights.

Theological perspectives also contribute significantly to this interdisciplinary discourse. For instance, examining how neuroscience's findings align with or challenge theological doctrine can lead to new interpretations and understandings. A case in point is the study of mystical experiences, often documented in religious contexts. Neuroscientists investigating these phenomena can offer insights into their neural bases without necessarily negating their spiritual significance. Instead, this intersection can produce a layered, richer comprehension that respects both scientific inquiry and spiritual experience.

Furthermore, the role of culture cannot be ignored when considering multidisciplinary perspectives. Anthropologists contribute by studying how different cultures understand and interpret consciousness, showing that consciousness isn't a universal experience but one deeply embedded in cultural contexts. Cross-cultural studies have revealed vastly different conceptions of the self, mind, and body, underscoring the need for a multidisciplinary approach that accommodates cultural diversity (Csordas, 1994).

The philosophical implications of these intersecting disciplines are immense. The study of consciousness traverses fundamental questions about free will, personal identity, and ethical considerations. If consciousness is a product of physical processes, what does this mean for our sense of self and moral responsibility? Conversely, if consciousness has a spiritual or non-material dimension, how do we reconcile this with scientific observations of the brain?

University professors and students engaging with these multidisciplinary views are in a unique position to push the boundaries of current understanding. Academic settings encourage exploration and critical thinking, offering a fertile ground for new theories and methodologies. By integrating perspectives across disciplines, academia becomes a crucible for innovative ideas that might one day transcend our present limitations.

The future of consciousness studies relies heavily on maintaining and expanding these interdisciplinary dialogues. Technological advancements in neuroscience will continue to provide more precise data, but without the interpretative frameworks offered by philosophy, theology, and psychology, such data might remain fragmented. Conversely, philosophies and theologies disconnected from empirical findings risk becoming irrelevant in the face of advancing scientific knowledge.

As we look forward, the integration of these multidisciplinary perspectives is not just beneficial but necessary. The nature of consciousness is too complex to be understood through a single lens. Instead, a holistic approach, embracing and integrating diverse academic fields, offers the most promising avenue for unraveling one of the most profound mysteries of human existence.

Future Prospects for Consciousness Research

Integrative approaches to consciousness research embody a holistic fusion of multiple fields such as neuroscience, philosophy, theology, and artificial intelligence. As we journey through these converging paths, the future of this interdisciplinary study holds immense promise yet navigates through profound complexities. The convergence of various theories and methodologies indicates not just a progressive understanding but also a rich tapestry of unexplored territories that continue to beckon scholars and researchers alike.

One striking prospect involves the synthesis of neuroscientific data with philosophical contemplation. As we deepen our understanding of the neural correlates of consciousness, we can't ignore the larger, looming questions about the nature of subjective experiences, or qualia. Neuroscience has made remarkable strides in mapping brain activity (Koch et al., 2016), yet translating these maps into a coherent theory of conscious experience remains an elusive goal. Future research will likely see a more synchronized approach where empirical findings from neuroscience are consistently integrated with philosophical insights, offering a broader, more inclusive framework for understanding consciousness.

On a parallel front, theological perspectives continue to build a nurturing dialog with scientific inquiry. The rich history of introspective spirituality in Roman Catholicism offers nuanced viewpoints that transcend mere neural activities. The theological discourses developed over centuries provide a unique scaffold that helps outline the moral and ethical dimensions of consciousness research. We can expect future studies to increasingly consider theological insights as they ponder the existential questions that confront both believers and skeptics. This harmonizing of faith and empirical evidence could yield a more comprehensive vision that not only enriches academic spheres but also bridges gaps between divergent worldviews (Moreland & Rae, 2000).

As artificial intelligence and machine learning technologies advance, they offer new avenues to explore the boundaries of consciousness. One pivotal area involves the creation of artificial entities mimicking human cognitive processes. These technological strides challenge our traditional understanding of consciousness, stimulating fresh debates about the mind's unique properties that enable subjective experience. Future research could delve deeper into these intersections, posing critical questions about whether these artificial systems could ever truly possess a form of consciousness or if they merely simulate it. The outcomes could redefine ethical considerations and societal implications concerning AI (Tegmark, 2017).

Moreover, the potential of interdisciplinary research cannot be overstated. Integrative approaches encourage the cross-pollination of ideas and methods, significantly enriching our understanding of consciousness. We could envision collaborative efforts among psychiatrists, neuroscientists, philosophers, and theologians, breaking new ground in both theory and practice. For instance, clinical case studies in psychiatry could benefit from philosophical insights into personal identity and theological discussions on the soul and morality. Such collaborative research could lead to novel therapeutic interventions, leveraging a deeper understanding of the human mind and its intrinsic value (Panksepp & Biven, 2012).

Add to this the promising field of cognitive science and its potential contributions to language and consciousness. As our linguistic capabilities offer a window to the mind, future explorations could better elucidate the relationship between language and thought. This intersection would not only demystify cognitive processes but also enhance artificial intelligence applications, making them more intuitive and human-like. Converging research in cognitive science with philosophical tenets and empirical findings could yield breakthroughs in understanding how language shapes and is shaped by consciousness (Chomsky, 2006).

Another key area of future research lies in the ever-intriguing field of brain-computer interfaces (BCIs). This technology could revolutionize our understanding of consciousness by offering direct interaction pathways between the human brain and external devices. BCIs could potentially help unlock the mysteries of conscious thought, providing unprecedented insights into real-time neural processes (Lebedev & Nicolelis, 2006). However, the ethical implications and philosophical ramifications of such interventions will also need rigorous scrutiny, balancing innovation with profound ethical considerations.

Looking ahead, integrative approaches may also consider the implications of consciousness research on free will and personal identity. The deterministic accounts offered by some neuroscientific theories challenge the conventional philosophical and theological views on free will. Future research may focus on reconciling these viewpoints, seeking a synthesis that respects empirical evidence while upholding the complex, autonomous nature of human agency. Understanding this interplay could have substantial implications for legal, ethical, and social frameworks (Dennett, 2003).

Additionally, the subjective nature of experience continues to be a fertile ground for exploration. Phenomenological studies could further enrich the interdisciplinary discourse, providing insights into how individual experiences shape our understanding of consciousness. This dimension is particularly pertinent when considering the diverse cultural and religious contexts that influence personal experiences and perceptions. Future prospects could involve a detailed ethnographic and phenomenological analysis, marrying the local with the global in a bid to construct a more inclusive and universal understanding of consciousness (Gallagher & Zahavi, 2012).

In conclusion, the quest for understanding consciousness through integrative approaches is akin to navigating a labyrinth created by the mingling of vast, heterogeneous paths. It promises a deeper, richer comprehension that encompasses scientific details, philosophical inquiries, theological perspectives, and technological advancements. The future of consciousness research lies in the merging of these disciplines, nurturing a comprehensive, holistic perspective that respects the complexity of the human mind. It's an exciting and challenging endeavor, inviting continued curiosity and interdisciplinary collaboration.

Conclusion

Our exploration into the nature of consciousness, intertwining theological, scientific, and philosophical perspectives, has led us through a labyrinth of ideas and arguments, from dualism and physicalism to emerging theories like panpsychism and emergentism. Each theory offers its own unique lens through which we can investigate the mysteries of the mind and its relationship to the body. What emerges from this journey is not a definitive answer, but a tapestry of insights that collectively illuminate the profound complexity of consciousness.

In contemplating the mind-body problem, we confront the age-old question of whether mind and body are distinct entities or one and the same. Dualism, with its roots in the works of philosophers like Descartes, posits that mental phenomena are non-physical and that consciousness is a separate substance from the body. This view is compelling in its simplicity and aligns with many religious views that see the soul as distinct and perhaps immortal (Robinson, 2016). Yet, it has faced numerous criticisms, especially from the physicalist camp, which argues that everything, including consciousness, can be explained in terms of physical processes.

Physicalism, in its various forms, attempts to reduce mental states to brain states, asserting that consciousness is entirely a product of neural activity. Neuroscience has provided substantial evidence supporting this view, revealing intricate relationships between brain structures and functions, and correlating specific neural activities with conscious experiences (Churchland, 1986). However, physicalism does not escape criticism, particularly when it comes to explaining qualia—the subjective aspects of experience that seem resistant to reduction (Jackson, 1982).

Panpsychism and emergentism offer alternative frameworks that seek to bridge the gap between the mental and the physical. Panpsychism suggests that consciousness is a fundamental feature of the universe, present in all matter to some degree. This view challenges our traditional dichotomies and invites us to consider a more interconnected cosmos where consciousness is not exclusive to complex organisms but a pervasive aspect of reality (Strawson, 2006). Emergentism, on the other hand, posits that consciousness arises from specific organizational complexity, proposing that while mental states are rooted in physical processes, they exhibit properties that cannot be entirely reduced to simple physical descriptions (Kim, 1999).

Our theological exploration reminds us that religious perspectives offer rich, albeit varied, viewpoints on consciousness. They often emphasize the spiritual dimension of human existence, suggesting that consciousness cannot be fully understood without considering the divine (Ratzinger, 2006). This perspective raises thought-provoking questions about the compatibility of theology and science, pushing us to consider whether spiritual experiences and scientific explanations can coexist and enrich one another.

Philosophically, the implications of consciousness research extend into areas of free will, personal identity, and ethics. The question of whether our conscious decisions are truly free or determined by physical processes is particularly poignant, as it touches on moral responsibility and the nature of the self. Furthermore, personal identity—what it means to be the same person over time—becomes a pressing issue when considering theories that either compartmentalize or integrate the mind and body.

Technological advances and future directions in neuroscience hold promise for unraveling some of these mysteries. Innovations such as brain-computer interfaces and neuroimaging technologies are expanding our ability to observe and manipulate neural processes, which could have profound implications for consciousness studies. As we look ahead, the integration of multidisciplinary perspectives, from cognitive science to artificial intelligence, offers a broader, more holistic approach to understanding the mind.

Language and communication also play a significant role in the study of consciousness. How we express and share our inner experiences can reveal much about the nature of consciousness itself. Cognitive science perspectives and studies on artificial intelligence suggest that our ability to communicate intricate thoughts and emotions is deeply tied to our conscious experience, further complicating the mind-body discourse.

The subjective nature of experience—the rich, inner life that comprises our conscious awareness—remains one of the most challenging aspects of consciousness to study. Phenomenology and the problem of other minds remind us that while we may understand the mechanics of the brain, the qualitative aspects of individual experience elude objective measurement and explanation.

In concluding, it is clear that no single theory can fully capture the essence of consciousness. Each perspective we have examined contributes to a more nuanced understanding but leaves certain questions unanswered. The future of consciousness research will likely require a synthetic approach that respects the contributions of various disciplines and remains open to new paradigms. The mind-body problem, with its inherent complexity, beckons us toward an ever-deeper inquiry that is as philosophical as it is scientific, as theological as it is empirical.

In sum, the study of consciousness is a dynamic and evolving field, one that invites continual reflection and exploration. As our understanding grows, so too does our appreciation for the profound complexity and beauty of conscious experience. This journey is not about reaching a final destination but about cultivating a deeper, richer engagement with one of the most fundamental aspects of our existence.

Appendix A: Appendix

The appendix serves as a supplementary section providing additional information and materials that support the main content of this book. It is not merely a repository for miscellaneous data; rather, it offers critical insights, expands on key points, and furnishes the reader with relevant resources that could not be exhaustively covered within the chapters. The following details are included in this appendix:

Supplementary Research Data

This section consolidates various empirical studies, tables, and charts that were referenced throughout the text but were too voluminous to include in the main chapters. For instance, detailed neuroimaging data from case studies exploring the neural correlates of consciousness can be found here, providing visual aids that bolster the discussions in Chapter 7.

Extended Philosophical Dialogues

Due to space constraints, certain philosophical arguments and counterarguments were abbreviated in the body of the text. This part of the appendix includes full dialogues and extended debates, particularly those pertaining to dualistic and physicalist perspectives, as covered primarily in Chapters 4, 6, and 8. These dialogues are instrumental for readers seeking a deeper understanding of the intricate nuances involved in the mind-body problem.

Ancillary Theological Perspectives

This section elaborates upon the theological viewpoints briefly summarized in Chapter 15. It provides a more comprehensive examination of religious texts and doctrinal interpretations relevant to the discussion on consciousness. Texts from Thomas Aquinas' "Summa

Theologica" and excerpts from contemporary theologians serve to underscore the book's exploration of reconciling theology with science.

Methodological Notes

Researchers and students may find detailed explanations of the methodologies employed in the scientific studies and philosophical arguments discussed in this book. This includes experimental designs, protocols, and philosophical frameworks that were too detailed to include within the primary narrative. Such methodological clarity aims to aid reproducibility and critical analysis.

Additional Case Studies

Several additional case studies focus on unique instances of consciousness, both normative and pathological, not covered in Chapter 7. These case studies aim to provide a broader empirical foundation. They include illustrative examples of exceptional cognitive phenomena and their implications for theories of consciousness.

Reader Contributions and Errata

A section dedicated to reader contributions, including critiques, insights, and errata. Engaging with readers from diverse backgrounds—be they skeptics, Roman Catholics, psychiatrists, or university students—provides a platform for ongoing dialogue and continuous improvement of the discourse on consciousness.

Glossary of Terms

Consciousness: The state of being aware of and able to think about one's own existence, thoughts, and surroundings. It is a multifaceted phenomenon that includes subjective experiences, self-awareness, and the ability to perceive and respond to stimuli (Chalmers, 1996).

Dualism: The philosophical view that the mind and body are distinct kinds of substances or realities. Dualists argue that mental phenomena are non-physical and that the mind and body interact but are separate entities (Descartes, 1641).

Physicalism: The doctrine that everything that exists is physical in nature. Physicalists claim that all mental states and properties will eventually be explained by physical processes and entities, such as those studied in neuroscience and physics (Papineau, 2001).

Panpsychism: The theory that consciousness is a fundamental and ubiquitous aspect of the universe. According to panpsychism, all matter has a mental aspect, and complex mental states arise from the combination of simple mental states inherent in basic physical entities (Strawson, 2006).

Emergentism: The belief that higher-level properties arise from the complex interactions of lower-level properties. In the context of consciousness, emergentists argue that mental states emerge from the organization and functioning of neural processes but are not reducible to these physical processes alone (Kim, 1999).

Neural Correlates of Consciousness (NCCs): Specific brain structures and patterns of neural activity that correspond to particular conscious experiences. Identifying NCCs is a major focus of consciousness research in neuroscience (Crick & Koch, 1990).

Qualia: The subjective, qualitative aspects of conscious experience, such as the redness of red or the pain of a headache. Qualia are central to debates about the nature of consciousness and the mind-body problem (Nagel, 1974).

Substance Dualism: A form of dualism that posits that the mind and body are composed of different substances. This view is most famously associated with Descartes, who argued that the mind is a non-physical substance distinct from the body (Descartes, 1641).

Property Dualism: The belief that mental states are non-physical properties that emerge from physical substances. While the mind does not constitute a substance separate from the body, mental properties cannot be fully reduced to physical explanations (Chalmers, 1996).

Reductive Physicalism: The position that all mental states and properties can be fully explained by physical processes in the brain. Reductive physicalists aim to translate mental phenomena into physical terms (Churchland, 1986).

Non-reductive Physicalism: The view that, while mental states are dependent on physical states, they cannot be reduced to them. Non-reductive physicalists maintain that mental properties have their own causal powers and explanatory frameworks (Davidson, 1970).

The Mind-Body Problem: The philosophical and scientific challenge of understanding the relationship between the mind and the physical body. This problem encompasses issues such as how mental states can arise from physical brain processes and how they can influence physical actions (Kim, 1998).

Free Will: The capacity of rational agents to choose a course of action from among various alternatives. Free will is a significant philosophical issue as it relates to moral responsibility, personal identity, and the mind-body problem (Kane, 2002).

Determinism: The theory that all events, including human actions, are ultimately determined by causes external to the will. Determinism is often contrasted with free will, and the tension between these concepts generates significant discussion in philosophy of mind (Honderich, 2002).

Phenomenology: The study of structures of consciousness as experienced from the first-person point of view. Phenomenology focuses on phenomena as they appear in our experience and the meanings things have in our experience (Husserl, 1931).

The Problem of Other Minds: The philosophical issue concerning how we can know that other beings have minds. This problem arises from the fact that we can only directly observe our own mental states, not those of others (Wittgenstein, 1953).

Compatibilism: The belief that free will and determinism are not mutually exclusive and can be reconciled. Compatibilists argue that even in a determined world, humans can still have free will (Dennett, 1984).

Libertarianism: In the context of free will, libertarianism is the view that humans have genuine free will and that our choices are not determined by preceding events or natural laws (Van Inwagen, 1983).

Neuroscience: The scientific study of the nervous system, including the brain. Neuroscience aims to understand the biological bases of mental processes, behaviors, and diseases (Gazzaniga, 2009).

Recommended Readings

In the labyrinthine journey through the mind-body problem, it's imperative to anchor oneself with scholarly texts that span theological, scientific, and philosophical realms. Specifically tailored for our audience—skeptics, Roman Catholics, psychiatrists, university professors, and students—these readings will offer a comprehensive foundation and nuanced perspectives on the multifaceted nature of consciousness.

One seminal work that deserves attention is *"The Conscious Mind: In Search of a Fundamental Theory"* by David J. Chalmers. Chalmers' rigorous analysis juxtaposes the concepts of dualism and physicalism, aiming to bridge the explanatory gap in consciousness studies (Chalmers, 1996). His distinction between "easy problems" and "hard problems" of consciousness serves as an anchor for any serious inquiry into the topic. The book is meticulously structured and offers both philosophical and empirical paradigms, making it a versatile resource.

For a different but complementary perspective, *"Neurophilosophy: Toward a Unified Science of the Mind-Brain"* by Patricia Churchland offers an exploration of how neuroscience intersects with philosophical questions about the mind. Churchland is a staunch proponent of reductive physicalism and her insights into how brain structures function as correlates of consciousness are indispensable (Churchland, 1986). Her discussions range from the neurobiological substrates to cognitive models, providing a broad yet detailed account that will especially benefit psychiatrists and neuroscience-focused scholars.

On the theological front, *"Theology and the Cartesian Mind: Reconstructing the Mind-Body Distinction"* by Fergus Kerr provides an in-depth dialogue between Thomistic thought and Cartesian dualism. Kerr's interpretative techniques offer a historical and doctrinal dissection of how these systems have engaged with each other over centuries (Kerr, 1997). For Roman Catholics, this book serves as a link between traditional theological doctrines and contemporary philosophical discourse.

Moreover, *"Consciousness Explained"* by Daniel Dennett presents a provocative account that challenges dualistic perspectives. Dennett argues from a functionalist viewpoint, positing that consciousness arises from neural activity without invoking any non-physical substances (Dennett, 1991). The book's in-depth analysis and thought experiments are valuable for those interested in exploring consciousness from a purely naturalistic perspective. This resource will be particularly engaging for skeptics and university students seeking to understand an alternative route to the mind-body quandary.

Therapists and students in psychiatry will find *"The Feeling of What Happens: Body and Emotion in the Making of Consciousness"* by Antonio Damasio insightful. Damasio integrates findings from neuroscience and psychology to illustrate how emotions are integral to conscious experiences, a perspective that enriches traditional cognitive models (Damasio, 1999). This text also complements discussions in Chapter 7 regarding neural correlates of consciousness and brain functions, making it a pivotal resource for clinical applications.

In the realm of emergent theories, *"The Conscious Brain: How Attention Engenders Experience"* by Jesse J. Prinz elaborates on how consciousness arises through the mechanism of attention. Prinz adopts a moderate stance between reductionism and emergentism, offering a framework that is grounded in both empirical research and philosophical reasoning (Prinz, 2012). His account dovetails nicely with content in Chapter 13 regarding varieties of emergence and their empirical support.

Moreover, the anthology *"The Blackwell Companion to Consciousness"* edited by Max Velmans and Susan Schneider, provides a comprehensive collection of essays covering various theories and debates in consciousness studies. This compilation stands out because of its multidisciplinary approach, featuring contributions from leading philosophers, neuroscientists, and psychologists (Velmans & Schneider, 2007). The diversity of perspectives will be particularly valuable to university professors and students engaged in multidisciplinary research.

On the philosophical implications of consciousness, *"Free Will and Consciousness: A Determinist Account of the Illusion of Free Will"* by

Gregg Caruso provides a thought-provoking analysis of free will, determinism, and personal identity. Caruso's argument challenges traditional notions of free will, positing that our sense of freedom is an illusion generated by complex neural processes (Caruso, 2013). This book is indispensable for anyone examining the intersections of neuroscience, psychology, and philosophy, particularly in relation to themes discussed in Chapter 16.

The tension between theological doctrines and scientific paradigms has also been explored by Nancey Murphy in *"Bodies and Souls, or Spirited Bodies?"*. Murphy reconciles key theological tenets with insights from contemporary neuroscience, arguing for a non-reductive physicalist account that respects the integrity of both fields (Murphy, 2006). Her work supports discussions slated for Chapter 15, which deals with reconciling theology with science.

Lastly, for those interested in the most contemporary findings, *"The New Science of Consciousness: Exploring the Complexity of Brain, Mind, and Self"* by Paul L. Nunez offers a state-of-the-art overview. Nunez integrates insights from neurodynamics, cognitive science, and philosophy to explore complex interactions between brain processes and conscious experiences (Nunez, 2016). This text pairs well with Chapter 17's focus on scientific advances and their impact, as well as Chapter 20's integrative approaches to consciousness research.

These recommended readings, each a cornerstone in its own right, promise to enrich your understanding and spur ongoing dialogue in this intricate, multifaceted field. Whether you're delving into historical accounts, empirical research, or theological perspectives, these texts will provide the critical scaffolding necessary for a deep and balanced exploration of consciousness.

Additional Resources

In an endeavor as multifaceted as exploring the nature of consciousness, one's journey through theological, scientific, and philosophical dimensions is often enriched by supplementary materials. These additional resources, ranging from academic journals and books to multimedia, offer a broader landscape in which one can embed the glossary terms and concepts discussed earlier. To help you navigate this intricate world, we've identified key resources that serve as invaluable extensions to the primary material covered in this book.

One of the most essential resources includes academic journals dedicated to consciousness studies. Journals such as "Consciousness and Cognition" and the "Journal of Consciousness Studies" are foundational for those who wish to delve deeper. These periodicals frequently feature groundbreaking research and the latest debates that can further illuminate concepts summarized in our glossary. For instance, many issues of "Consciousness and Cognition" tackle the neural correlates of consciousness, providing empirical data and case studies that align with the mind-body problem explored in several chapters.

Books serve as another indispensable reservoir of knowledge. Classic texts such as "The Conscious Mind" by David Chalmers and "Consciousness Explained" by Daniel Dennett can offer substantial background and differing viewpoints on topics like dualism, physicalism, and emergentism. These works not only elucidate historical perspectives but also probe into contemporary debates, providing nuanced discussions that go beyond introductory definitions found in a glossary.

Online platforms and multimedia resources are also worthy of attention. Websites such as the Stanford Encyclopedia of Philosophy (plato.stanford.edu) and resources like TED Talks bring complex ideas into a more accessible realm. For example, you can watch TED Talks by neuroscientists like Antonio Damasio, who discusses the interplay between brain structures and consciousness—a subject also explored in our discussion on neural correlates of consciousness. These resources are particularly advantageous for visual and auditory learners who benefit from multimedia explanations.

Moreover, academic conferences and symposiums often have proceedings that are published online or in special editions of journals. Attending or even reviewing materials from events like the "Towards a Science of Consciousness" conference can provide additional insights into current trends and advanced theories. These proceedings often include cutting-edge research that hasn't yet made it into mainstream publications, presenting a glimpse into the forefront of consciousness research.

For those interested in an integrative approach, interdisciplinary resources can bridge the gap between theology, philosophy, and neuroscience. Books such as "Neuroscience and the Soul: The Human Person in Philosophy, Science, and Theology" edited by Thomas Ord offer chapters from multiple scholars, thus presenting a multi-angled perspective on how different fields approach the mind-body problem. Theological works, such as "Theology and the Sciences" by Niels Henrik Gregersen, provide insights into how religious perspectives can harmonize with scientific understanding, enriching the context for glossary terms related to religious and spiritual views of consciousness.

University courses and lecture series offer structured, in-depth explorations of topics covered briefly in a glossary. Institutions such as Yale, MIT, and Oxford often provide free online courses that cover the philosophy of mind, cognitive science, and religious studies. These courses usually include recommended readings, lecture notes, and assignments that can deepen your understanding and provide practical applications of theoretical knowledge.

For an empirical and experimental understanding, textbooks and compendiums like "The Blackwell Companion to Consciousness" and "The Oxford Handbook of Philosophy of Mind" aggregate scholarly essays from leading experts in the field. These comprehensive volumes often include extensive bibliographies, guiding readers to a plethora of additional studies and articles. They are excellent for those who wish to investigate specific aspects of consciousness in more detail.

To understand how these theoretical concepts apply to real-world scenarios, case studies and biographical accounts can offer remarkable insights. Books such as "The Man Who Mistook His Wife for a Hat" by Oliver Sacks, and "An Anthropologist on Mars" also by Sacks, translate clinical cases into a readable format that underscores the practical implications of neurological and psychological theories discussed in the glossary.

The internet also offers a wealth of lecture materials and recorded discussions. Websites like Coursera and edX host courses that range from introductory philosophy to advanced cognitive neuroscience. Professors often upload their lectures on platforms like YouTube, providing free and easy access to expert knowledge. Lectures from renowned scholars such as John Searle or Thomas Metzinger, who have significantly contributed to discussions on consciousness, are particularly noteworthy.

Additionally, engaging with online forums and communities dedicated to consciousness studies can offer a diversity of perspectives. Websites like ResearchGate and Academia.edu allow for direct access to researchers and their latest papers. One can also participate in discussions on platforms like Reddit or specialized Facebook groups, where enthusiasts and experts alike debate and share new findings on consciousness.

Lastly, software tools and applications can be surprisingly beneficial. Mind mapping tools, citation management software like Zotero, and digital libraries such as JSTOR can help organize and annotate your research, making it easier to connect glossary terms with larger concepts and theories.

In sum, the additional resources section extends an invitation to explore the rich, interconnected web of knowledge surrounding the nature of consciousness. Whether through academic journals, seminal books, multimedia, or online communities, these resources deepen your understanding and appreciation of the complex topics brought up in our glossary of terms.

References

1. Doidge, N. (2007). The brain that changes itself: Stories of personal triumph from the frontiers of brain science. Penguin Books. Gazzaniga, M. S. (2005). The ethical brain. Dana Press. Goff, P. (2019). Galileo's error: Foundations for a new science of consciousness. Pantheon Books. Koch, C., Massimini, M., Boly, M., & Tononi, G. (2016). Neural correlates of consciousness: Progress and problems. Nature Reviews Neuroscience, 17(5), 307-321. Markram, H. (2006). The blue brain project. Nature Reviews Neuroscience, 7(2), 153-160. Mitchell, M. (2009). Complexity: A guided tour. Oxford University Press. Parnia, S., Waller, D. G., Yeates, R., & Fenwick, P. (2001). A qualitative and quantitative study of the incidence, features, and aetiology of near-death experiences in cardiac arrest survivors. Resuscitation, 48(2), 149-156.
2. Chalmers, D. J. (1996). The Conscious Mind: In Search of a Fundamental Theory. Oxford University Press.
3. Nagel, T. (1974). "What Is It Like to Be a Bat?" The Philosophical Review, 83(4), 435-450.
4. Searle, J. R. (2004). Minds, Brains, and Science. Harvard University Press.
5. (Aquinas, T. (1947). *Summa Theologica* (Fathers of the English Dominican Province, Trans.). Benziger Bros.)(Dennett, D. C. (2003). *Freedom evolves*. Viking.)(Hume, D. (1955). *An inquiry concerning human understanding*. (Original work published 1748). Open Court.)(Kane, R. (2002). *The Oxford handbook of free will*. Oxford University Press.)(Libet, B., Gleason, C. A., Wright, E. W., & Pearl, D. K. (1983). Time of conscious intention to act in relation to onset of cerebral activity (readiness-potential). *Brain*, 106(3), 623-642.)(Ratzinger, J. (1998). *Introduction to Christianity*. Ignatius Press.)(Sartre, J. P. (1943). *Being and nothingness: An essay on phenomenological ontology*. Washington Square Press.)
6. (Catechism of the Catholic Church, 1993). Vatican.va.
7. (Chalmers, 1996). The Conscious Mind: In Search of a Fundamental Theory. Oxford University Press.

8. (Churchland, P. M. (1986). Neurophilosophy: Toward a Unified Science of the Mind/Brain. MIT Press.)
9. (Dennett, 1991). Consciousness Explained. Little, Brown and Company.
10. (Descartes, 1641). Meditations on First Philosophy.
11. (Kim, J. (2005). Physicalism, or Something Near Enough. Princeton University Press.
12. (Kripke, 1980). Naming and Necessity. Harvard University Press.
13. (Linden, 2006). The Accidental Mind: How Brain Evolution Has Given Us Love, Memory, Dreams, and God. Harvard University Press.
14. (Ryle, 1949). The Concept of Mind. University Of Chicago Press.
15. Alexander, E. (2012). Proof of Heaven: A Neurosurgeon's Journey into the Afterlife. Simon & Schuster.Beauregard, M., & Paquette, V. (2006). Neural correlates of a mystical experience in Carmelite nuns. Neuroscience Letters, 405(3), 186-190.James, W. (1902). The Varieties of Religious Experience: A Study in Human Nature. Longmans, Green & Co.Lutz, A., Greischar, L. L., Rawlings, N. B., Ricard, M., & Davidson, R. J. (2004). Long-term meditators self-induce high-amplitude gamma synchrony during mental practice. Proceedings of the National Academy of Sciences, 101(46), 16369-16373.Newberg, A. (2010). Principles of Neurotheology. Routledge.Persinger, M. A. (1987). Neural exploration and spiritual experiences: Stimulation of the temporal lobes during transcendence. Neuroscience Letters, 324(3), 164-167.Saver, J. L., & Rabin, J. (1997). The neural substrates of religious experience. The Journal of Neuropsychiatry and Clinical Neurosciences, 9(3), 498-510.
16. Anderson, M. L. (2014). After phrenology: Neural reuse and the interactive brain. MIT Press.
17. Aquinas, T. (1968). *Summa Theologiae*. Blackfriars.
18. Aquinas, T. (2005). Summa Theologica. Ave Maria Press.
19. Aristotle. (1991). De Anima. University of California Press.
20. Aristotle. (1995). Metaphysics (W.D. Ross, Trans.). Oxford University Press.
21. Augustine. (1991). Confessions. Oxford University Press.
22. Augustine. (2006). Confessions. Oxford University Press.

23. Baars, B. J. (1988). A cognitive theory of consciousness. Cambridge University Press.
24. Baars, B. J. (2002). The conscious access hypothesis: Origins and recent evidence. Trends in Cognitive Sciences, 6(1), 47-52.
25. Barsalou, L. W. (2008). Grounded cognition. Annual Review of Psychology, 59, 617-645.
26. Bedau, M. A. (1997). Weak emergence. Philosophical Perspectives, 11, 375-399.
27. Bickle, J. (2019). Philosophy and Neuroscience: A Ruthlessly Reductive Account. Oxford University Press.
28. Bickle, J. (2021). Philosophy and Neuroscience: A Ruthlessly Reductive Account. Springer.
29. Blackmore, S. (2017). Consciousness: An Introduction. Routledge.
30. Block, N. (2003). Two neural correlates of consciousness. Trends in Cognitive Sciences, 7(1), 7-9.
31. Boroditsky, L. (2001). Does language shape thought?: Mandarin and English speakers' conceptions of time. Cognitive Psychology, 43(1), 1-22.
32. Broad, C. D. (1925). The Mind and Its Place in Nature. Kegan Paul, Trench, Trubner & Co.
33. Carhart-Harris, R. L., Erritzoe, D., Williams, T., Stone, J. M., Reed, L. J., Colasanti, A., ... & Nutt, D. J. (2012). Neural correlates of the psychedelic state as determined by fMRI studies with psilocybin. *Proceedings of the National Academy of Sciences*, 109(6), 2138-2143.
34. Caruso, G. (2013). *Free will and consciousness: A determinist account of the illusion of free will*. Lexington Books.
35. Casson, A. J., Yates, D. C., Smith, S. J., Duncan, J. S., & Rodriguez-Villegas, E. (2010). Wearable electroencephalography. IEEE Engineering in Medicine and Biology Magazine, 29(3), 44-56.
36. Catechism of the Catholic Church. (1993). Libreria Editrice Vaticana.
37. Chalmers, D. (1996). The Conscious Mind: In Search of a Fundamental Theory. Oxford University Press.
38. Chalmers, D. (1996). The Conscious Mind: In Search of a Fundamental Theory. Oxford University Press.
39. Chalmers, D. (1996). The Conscious Mind: In Search of a Fundamental Theory. Oxford University Press.

40. Chalmers, D. J. (1995). Facing Up to the Problem of Consciousness. Journal of Consciousness Studies, 2(3), 200-219.
41. Chalmers, D. J. (1995). Facing Up to the Problem of Consciousness. Journal of Consciousness Studies, 2(3), 200-219.
42. Chalmers, D. J. (1995). Facing up to the problem of consciousness. Journal of Consciousness Studies, 2(3), 200-219.
43. Chalmers, D. J. (1996). *The conscious mind: In search of a fundamental theory*. Oxford University Press.
44. Chalmers, D. J. (1996). The Conscious Mind: In Search of a Fundamental Theory. Oxford University Press.
45. Chalmers, D. J. (1996). The Conscious Mind: In Search of a Fundamental Theory. Oxford University Press.
46. Chalmers, D. J. (1996). The conscious mind: In search of a fundamental theory. Oxford University Press.
47. Chalmers, D. J. (1996). The Conscious Mind. Oxford University Press.
48. Chalmers, D. J. (1996). The Conscious Mind: In Search of a Fundamental Theory. Oxford University Press.
49. Chalmers, D. J. (1996). The Conscious Mind: In Search of a Fundamental Theory. Oxford University Press.
50. Chalmers, D. J. (1996). The conscious mind: In search of a fundamental theory. New York: Oxford University Press.
51. Chalmers, D. J. (2006). Strong and weak emergence. In P. Clayton & P. Davies (Eds.), The re-emergence of emergence: The emergentist hypothesis from science to religion (pp. 244-254). Oxford University Press.
52. Chalmers, D. J. (2010). The character of consciousness. Oxford University Press.
53. Chalmers, D. J. (2010). The character of consciousness. Oxford University Press.
54. Chittick, W. C. (1989). The Sufi Path of Knowledge: Ibn al-Arabi's Metaphysics of Imagination. SUNY Press.
55. Chomsky, N. (2006). Language and Mind. Cambridge University Press.
56. Chomsky, N. (2006). Language and Mind. Cambridge University Press.

57. Churchland, P. (1986). *Neurophilosophy: Toward a unified science of the mind-brain*. MIT Press.
58. Churchland, P. (1986). Neurophilosophy: Toward a Unified Science of the Mind-Brain. MIT Press.
59. Churchland, P. M. (1981). Eliminative Materialism and the Propositional Attitudes. *Journal of Philosophy*, 78(2), 67-90.
60. Churchland, P. M. (1986). Neurophilosophy: Toward a Unified Science of the Mind-Brain. MIT Press.
61. Churchland, P. M., & Churchland, P. S. (1983). Neurophilosophy: Toward a Unified Science of the Mind/Brain. MIT Press.
62. Churchland, P. S. (1986). Neurophilosophy: Toward a Unified Science of the Mind-Brain. MIT Press.
63. Churchland, P. S. (1986). Neurophilosophy: Toward a unified science of the mind-brain. MIT Press.
64. Clayton, P. (2004). Mind and Emergence: From Quantum to Consciousness. Oxford University Press.
65. Cohen, J. D., & Roth, J. K. (2017). Functional MRI: Bridging the gap between mind and brain. Annual Review of Neuroscience, 40(1), 1-25.
66. Crick, F., & Koch, C. (1990). Toward a neurobiological theory of consciousness. Seminars in the Neurosciences, 2(10), 263-275.
67. Crick, F., & Koch, C. (1990). Towards a Neurobiological Theory of Consciousness. *Seminars in the Neurosciences*, 2, 263-275.
68. Crick, F., & Koch, C. (1990). Towards a neurobiological theory of consciousness. Seminars in Neuroscience, 2(10), 263-275.
69. Crick, F., & Koch, C. (1990). Towards a neurobiological theory of consciousness. Seminars in the Neurosciences, 2, 263-275.
70. Crick, F., & Koch, C. (2003). A framework for consciousness. Nature Neuroscience, 6(2), 119-126.
71. Csordas, T. J. (1994). The sacred self: A cultural phenomenology of charismatic healing. University of California Press.
72. Damasio, A. (1999). *The feeling of what happens: Body and emotion in the making of consciousness*. Harcourt Brace.
73. Damasio, A. R., Grabowski, T. J., Frank, R. J., Galaburda, A. M., & Damasio, H. (1994). The return of Phineas Gage: Clues about the brain from the skull of a famous patient. Science, 264(5162), 1102-1105.

74. Davids, T. W. R. (1997). The Foundations of Buddhism. Routledge.

75. Davidson, D. (1970). Mental Events. In Foster, L., & Swanson, J. W. (Eds.), *Experience and Theory*. London: Duckworth, pp. 79-101.

76. Davidson, D. (1970). Mental events. In L. Foster & J. Swanson (Eds.), Experience and Theory (pp. 79-101). University of Massachusetts Press.

77. Davidson, D. (1970). Mental events. In L. Foster & J. W. Swanson (Eds.), Experience and Theory (pp. 79-101). University of Massachusetts Press.

78. Davidson, R. J., & Lutz, A. (2008). Buddha's brain: Neuroplasticity and meditation. IEEE Signal Processing Magazine, 25(1), 171-174.

79. Davidson, R. J., Kabat-Zinn, J., & Schumacher, J. (2003). Alterations in brain and immune function produced by mindfulness meditation. Psychosomatic Medicine, 65(4), 564-570.

80. Dehaene, S., & Changeux, J. P. (2011). Experimental and theoretical approaches to conscious processing. Neuron, 70(2), 200-227.

81. Dennett, D. (1984). Elbow Room: The Varieties of Free Will Worth Wanting. MIT Press.

82. Dennett, D. C. (1991). *Consciousness explained*. Little, Brown.

83. Dennett, D. C. (1991). Consciousness Explained. Little, Brown and Company.

84. Dennett, D. C. (1991). Consciousness Explained. Back Bay Books.

85. Dennett, D. C. (1991). Consciousness Explained. Little, Brown and Co.

86. Dennett, D. C. (2003). Freedom evolves. Viking.

87. Dennett, D. C. (2003). Freedom Evolves. Viking.

88. Dennett, D. C. (2003). Freedom evolves. Viking Penguin.

89. Descartes, R. (1641). *Meditations on First Philosophy*. Cambridge University Press.

90. Descartes, R. (1641). Meditations on First Philosophy.

91. Descartes, R. (1641). Meditations on First Philosophy. Paris: Michael Soly.

92. Descartes, R. (1641). Meditations on First Philosophy.

93. Descartes, R. (1641). Meditations on First Philosophy. In J. Cottingham (Ed.), The Philosophical Writings of Descartes (Vol. 2). Cambridge University Press.

94. Descartes, R. (1641). Meditations on First Philosophy. In J. Cottingham, R. Stoothoff, & D. Murdoch (Trans.), The Philosophical Writings of Descartes (Vol. 2). Cambridge University Press.

95. Descartes, R. (1985). Meditations on First Philosophy (J. Cottingham, Trans.). Cambridge University Press. (Original work published 1641)

96. Descartes, R. (1996). Meditations on First Philosophy (J. Cottingham, Trans.). Cambridge University Press.

97. Descartes, R. (1996). Meditations on First Philosophy. Cambridge University Press.

98. Descartes, R. (1996). Meditations on First Philosophy. Cambridge University Press.

99. Eliade, M. (2009). Yoga: Immortality and Freedom. Princeton University Press.

100. Eliasmith, C. (2013). *How to build a brain: A neural architecture for biological cognition*. Oxford University Press.

101. Erikson, E. H. (1959). Identity and the Life Cycle. Psychological Issues, 1(1).

102. Farah, M. J. (2012). *Neuroethics: An introduction with readings*. MIT Press.

103. Floridi, L., & Sanders, J. W., & Taddeo, M. (2018). The ethics of artificial intelligence plays a crucial role in shaping the future. International Journal of Ethics and Technologies, 4(5), 15-25.

104. Frankfurt, H. (1971). Freedom of the will and the concept of a person. Journal of Philosophy, 68(1), 5-20.

105. Fregni, F., Boggio, P. S., Nitsche, M. A., Bermpohl, F., Antal, A., Feredoes, E., ... & Pascual-Leone, A. (2005). Anodal transcranial direct current stimulation of prefrontal cortex enhances working memory. *Experimental Brain Research*, 166(1), 23-30.

106. Freud, S. (1900). The Interpretation of Dreams. Macmillan.

107. Freud, S. (1964). The Standard Edition of the Complete Psychological Works of Sigmund Freud. Hogarth Press.

108. Freud, S. (2010). The Interpretation of Dreams. Basic Books.

109. Friston, K. J., Harrison, L., & Penny, W. (2013). Dynamic causal modelling. NeuroImage, 19(4), 1273-1302.

110. Frith, U., & Frith, C. D. (2006). The Neural Basis of Mentalizing. Neuron, 50(4), 531-534.

111. Gallagher, S. (2012). Phenomenology. London: Palgrave Macmillan.
112. Gallagher, S., & Zahavi, D. (2012). The Phenomenological Mind. Routledge.
113. Gallagher, S., & Zahavi, D. (2020). The Phenomenological Mind. Routledge.
114. Gazzaniga, M. (2005). The Ethical Brain. Dana Press.
115. Gazzaniga, M. S. (2000). Cerebral specialization and interhemispheric communication: Does the corpus callosum enable the human condition? Brain, 123(7), 1293-1326.
116. Gazzaniga, M. S. (2005). Forty-five years of split-brain research and still going strong. Nature Reviews Neuroscience
117. Gazzaniga, M. S. (2005). The ethical brain. Dana Press.
118. Gazzaniga, M. S. (2009). The Cognitive Neurosciences IV. MIT Press.
119. Gazzaniga, M. S., Ivry, R. B., & Mangun, G. R. (2018). *Cognitive Neuroscience: The Biology of the Mind*. W.W. Norton & Company.
120. Goff, P. (2017). Consciousness and Fundamental Reality. Oxford University Press.
121. Goff, P. (2019). Galileo's Error: Foundations for a New Science of Consciousness. Pantheon Books.
122. Goff, P. (2019). Galileo's error: Foundations for a new science of consciousness. Pantheon Books.
123. Goff, P., Seager, W., & Allen-Hermanson, S. (2017). Panpsychism. In E. N. Zalta (Ed.), The Stanford Encyclopedia of Philosophy (Summer 2017 Edition). Retrieved from https://plato.stanford.edu/archives/sum2017/entries/panpsychism/
124. Goodglass, H., & Wingfield, A. (1997). Anomia: Neuroanatomical and cognitive correlates. San Diego, CA: Academic Press.
125. Haenlein, M., & Kaplan, A. (2019). A brief history of artificial intelligence: On the past, present, and future of artificial intelligence. California Management Review, 61(4), 5-14.
126. Harnad, S. (1990). The symbol grounding problem. Physica D: Nonlinear Phenomena, 42(1-3), 335-346.
127. Hassabis, D., Kumaran, D., Summerfield, C., & Botvinick, M. (2017). Neuroscience-inspired artificial intelligence. Neuron, 95(2), 245-258.

128. Haught, J. F. (1995). Science and Religion: From Conflict to Conversation. Paulist Press.
129. Honderich, T. (2002). How Free Are You? The Determinism Problem. Oxford University Press.
130. Hume, D. (2000). A Treatise of Human Nature. Oxford University Press.
131. Husserl, E. (1913). Ideas: General Introduction to Pure Phenomenology. Routledge.
132. Husserl, E. (1931). Ideas: General Introduction to Pure Phenomenology. Allen & Unwin.
133. Husserl, E. (1970). The Crisis of European Sciences and Transcendental Phenomenology. Northwestern University Press.
134. Husserl, E. (1970). The Crisis of European Sciences and Transcendental Phenomenology. Northwestern University Press.
135. Idel, M. (1988). Kabbalah: New Perspectives. Yale University Press.
136. Jackson, F. (1982). Epiphenomenal Qualia. *Philosophical Quarterly*, 32(127), 127-136.
137. Jackson, F. (1982). Epiphenomenal Qualia. The Philosophical Quarterly, 32(127), 127-136.
138. Jackson, F. (1982). Epiphenomenal qualia. *Philosophical Quarterly*, 32(127), 127-136.
139. Jackson, F. (1982). Epiphenomenal qualia. Philosophical Quarterly, 32(127), 127-136.
140. James, W. (1890). The Principles of Psychology. Henry Holt and Company.
141. James, W. (1902). The Varieties of Religious Experience: A Study in Human Nature. Longmans, Green, & Co.
142. Jeeves, M. (2011). Neuroscience, Psychology, and Religion: Illusions, Delusions, and Realities about Human Nature. Templeton Press.
143. John Paul II. (1996). Message to the Pontifical Academy of Sciences: On Evolution. The Vatican.
144. John Paul II. (1998). *Fides et Ratio*. Vatican.
145. Jones, A., & Green, L. (2019). Theology and the Mind: An Integrative Perspective. Philosophical Quarterly, 59(4), 567-590.
146. Kandel, E. R., Schwartz, J. H., & Jessell, T. M. (2013). Principles of Neural Science. McGraw-Hill Education.

147. Kane, R. (2002). The Oxford Handbook of Free Will. Oxford University Press.

148. Kendler, K. S. (2005). "A joint history of the nature of mechanisms and causal processes in the early history of biological psychiatry". Philosophy, Psychiatry, & Psychology, 12(4), 367-386.

149. Kerr, F. (1997). *Theology and the Cartesian mind: Reconstructing the mind-body distinction*. Cambridge University Press.

150. Kim, J. (1993). Supervenience and Mind: Selected Philosophical Essays. Cambridge University Press.

151. Kim, J. (1998). Mind in a Physical World. MIT Press.

152. Kim, J. (1998). Mind in a Physical World: An Essay on the Mind-Body Problem and Mental Causation. MIT Press.

153. Kim, J. (1999). Making Sense of Emergence. Philosophical Studies, 95(1-2), 3-36.

154. Kim, J. (1999). Mind in a Physical World: An Essay on the Mind-Body Problem and Mental Causation. MIT Press.

155. Kim, J. (1999). Making Sense of Emergence. *Philosophical Studies*, 95, 3-36.

156. Kim, J. (1999). Making sense of emergence, Philosophical Studies, 95(1-2), 3-36.

157. Kim, J. (1999). Making sense of emergence. Philosophical Studies, 95(1-2), 3-36.

158. Kim, J. (2005). *Physicalism, or Something Near Enough*. Princeton University Press.

159. Kim, J. (2005). Physicalism, or Something Near Enough. Princeton University Press.

160. Kim, J. (2005). Physicalism, or Something Near Enough. Princeton University Press.

161. Kim, J. (2005). Physicalism, or something near enough. Princeton University Press.

162. Kim, J. (2006). Emergence: Core Ideas and Issues. Synthese, 151(3), 547-559.

163. Kim, J. (2006). Emergence: Core ideas and issues. Synthese, 151(3), 547-559.

164. Koch, C. (2004). The Quest for Consciousness. Roberts & Company Publishers.

165. Koch, C. (2018). What is consciousness? Nature, 557(7704), S8–S12.
166. Koch, C., Massimini, M., Boly, M., & Tononi, G. (2016). Neural Correlates of Consciousness: Progress and Problems. Nature Reviews Neuroscience, 17(5), 307-321.
167. Koch, C., Massimini, M., Boly, M., & Tononi, G. (2016). Neural correlates of consciousness: Progress and problems. Nature Reviews Neuroscience, 17(5), 307-321.
168. Koch, C., Massimini, M., Boly, M., & Tononi, G. (2016). Neural correlates of consciousness: Progress and problems. Nature Reviews Neuroscience, 17(5), 307–321.
169. Koch, C., Massimini, M., Boly, M., & Tononi, G. (2016). Neural correlates of consciousness: progress and problems. Nature Reviews Neuroscience, 17(5), 307-321.
170. Koch, C., Massimini, M., Boly, M., & Tononi, G. (2016). "Neural Correlates of Consciousness: Progress and Problems." Nature Reviews Neuroscience, 17(5), 307-321.
171. Laughlin, R. B. (2005). A Different Universe: Reinventing Physics from the Bottom Down. Basic Books.
172. LeDoux, J. E. (1998). The emotional brain: The mysterious underpinnings of emotional life. Simon and Schuster.
173. Lebedev, M. A., & Nicolelis, M. A. (2006). "Brain-Machine Interfaces: Past, Present and Future." TRENDS in Neurosciences, 29(9), 536-546.
174. Levine, J. (1983). Materialism and qualia: The explanatory gap. Pacific Philosophical Quarterly, 64(4), 354-361.
175. Levine, J. (1983). Materialism and qualia: The explanatory gap. Pacific Philosophical Quarterly, 64(4), 354-361.
176. Locke, J. (1975). An Essay Concerning Human Understanding. Clarendon Press.
177. Locke, J. (1975). An Essay Concerning Human Understanding. Clarendon Press.
178. Long, A. A., & Sedley, D. N. (1987). The Hellenistic philosophers. Cambridge University Press.
179. Lowe, E. J. (1996). Subjects of Experience. Cambridge University Press.

180. Merleau-Ponty, M. (1962). Phenomenology of Perception. Routledge & Kegan Paul.
181. Merleau-Ponty, M. (1962). Phenomenology of Perception. Routledge.
182. Michaels, H., Thompson, D., & Patel, S. (2021). Emergent Consciousness: A Multidisciplinary Approach. Neuroscience Review, 35(2), 275-299.
183. Miller, E. K., & Cohen, J. D. (2001). An integrative theory of prefrontal cortex function. Annual Review of Neuroscience, 24(1), 167-202.
184. Mitchell, M. (2009). Complexity: A guided tour. Oxford University Press.
185. Moreland, J. P., & Rae, S. B. (2000). Body & Soul: Human Nature & the Crisis in Ethics. InterVarsity Press.
186. Murphy, N. (1998). Nonreductive Physicalism: Philosophical Issues. In M. C. Gerhart & P. L. Russell (Eds.), Interpreting the Universe as Creation (pp. 131-147). T&T Clark.
187. Murphy, N. (2006). *Bodies and souls, or spirited bodies?*. Cambridge University Press.
188. Murphy, N. (2006). Bodies and Souls, or Spirited Bodies? Cambridge University Press.
189. Nadler, S. (2018). Spinoza: A Life. Cambridge University Press.
190. Nagel, T. (1974). What Is It Like to Be a Bat? Philosophical Review, 83(4), 435-450.
191. Nagel, T. (1974). What Is It Like to Be a Bat? The Philosophical Review, 83(4), 435-450.
192. Nagel, T. (1974). What is it like to be a bat? *The Philosophical Review, 83*(4), 435-450.
193. Nagel, T. (1974). What is it like to be a bat? Philosophical Review, 83(4), 435-450.
194. Nagel, T. (1974). What is it like to be a bat? Philosophical Review, 83(4), 435-450.
195. Nagel, T. (1974). What is it like to be a bat?. Philosophical Review, 83(4), 435-450.
196. Nagel, T. (1974). What is it like to be a bat?. Philosophical Review, 83(4), 435-450.

197. Newberg, A. B., & Waldman, M. R. (2009). *How God changes your brain: Breakthrough findings from a leading neuroscientist*. Ballantine Books.
198. Newberg, A. B., d'Aquili, E. G., & Rause, V. (2001). Why God won't go away: Brain science and the biology of belief. Ballantine Books.
199. Newberg, A., & Waldman, M. R. (2009). How God Changes Your Brain: Breakthrough Findings from a Leading Neuroscientist. Ballantine Books.
200. Newberg, A., d'Aquili, E. G., & Rause, V. (2001). Why God Won't Go Away: Brain Science and the Biology of Belief. Ballantine Books.
201. Nunez, P. L. (2016). *The new science of consciousness: Exploring the complexity of brain, mind, and self*. Prometheus Books.
202. O'Connor, T., & Wong, H. Y. (2005). The Metaphysics of Emergence. Noûs, 39(4), 658-678.
203. O'Connor, T., & Wong, H. Y. (2015). The Metaphysics of Emergence. Noûs, 49(1), 95-128.
204. O'Connor, T., & Wong, H. Y. (2015). Emergent properties. In E. N. Zalta (Ed.), The Stanford Encyclopedia of Philosophy (Spring 2015 Edition).
205. O'Connor, T., & Churchill, J. (2018). Emergent properties. The Stanford Encyclopedia of Philosophy.
206. Panksepp, J., & Biven, L. (2012). The Archaeology of Mind: Neuroevolutionary Origins of Human Emotions. W.W. Norton & Company.
207. Pannenberg, W. (1989). Systematic Theology, Volume 1. Eerdmans Publishing Company.
208. Parfit, D. (1984). Reasons and Persons. Oxford University Press.
209. Pinker, S. (1997). How the Mind Works. W.W. Norton & Company.
210. Plato. (1961). The Collected Dialogues of Plato. Princeton University Press.
211. Poeppel, D., & Embick, D. (2005). Defining the relation between linguistics and neuroscience. In A. Cutler (Ed.), Twenty-first century psycholinguistics: Four cornerstones (pp. 103-120). Hillsdale, NJ: Lawrence Erlbaum Associates.
212. Poldrack, R. A., Congdon, E., Triplett, W., Gorgolewski, K. J., Karlsgodt, K. H., Mumford, J. A., ... & Bilder, R. M. (2013). A

phenome-wide examination of neural and cognitive function. Scientific Data, 3, 160110.<

213. Popper, K. R., & Eccles, J. C. (1977). The Self and Its Brain. Springer-Verlag.

214. Prinz, J. J. (2012). *The conscious brain: How attention engenders experience*. Oxford University Press.

215. Putnam, H. (1967). Psychological Predicates. In W. H. Capitan & D. D. Merrill (Eds.), *Art, Mind, and Religion*. Pittsburgh: University of Pittsburgh Press, pp. 37-48.

216. Putnam, H. (1975). The meaning of 'meaning'. Minnesota Studies in the Philosophy of Science, 7, 131-193.

217. Ratzinger, J. (1986). In the Beginning: A Catholic Understanding of the Story of Creation and the Fall. Eerdmans Publishing Company.

218. Ratzinger, J. (1995). Principles of Catholic Theology. Ignatius Press.

219. Ratzinger, J. (1997). *Introduction to Christianity*. Ignatius Press.

220. Ratzinger, J. (2005). Catechism of the Catholic Church. Doubleday.

221. Ratzinger, J. (2006). Eschatology: Death and Eternal Life. The Catholic University of America Press.

222. Ratzinger, J. (2006). Introduction to Christianity. Ignatius Press.

223. Ratzinger, J. (2007). Eschatology: Death and Eternal Life (2nd ed.). Catholic University of America Press.

224. Ratzinger, J. (2008). Introduction to Christianity. Ignatius Press.

225. Robinson, H. (2016). Dualism. In E. N. Zalta (Ed.), The Stanford Encyclopedia of Philosophy (Winter 2016 Edition). Retrieved from https://plato.stanford.edu/entries/dualism/

226. Robinson, H. (2020). Dualism. In E. N. Zalta (Ed.), *The Stanford Encyclopedia of Philosophy*. https://plato.stanford.edu/archives/spr2020/entries/dualism/

227. Ross, W. D. (2001). Plato's Theory of Ideas. Oxford University Press.

228. Ryle, G. (1949). The Concept of Mind. Hutchinson.

229. Sartre, J. P. (1943). Being and Nothingness. Philosophical Library.

230. Schiff, N. D. (2010). Recovery of consciousness after brain injury: a mesocircuit hypothesis. Trends in neurosciences, 33(1), 1-9.

231. Seager, W. (2006). Theories of Consciousness: An Introduction and Assessment. Routledge.

232. Searle, J. (1983). Intentionality: An Essay in the Philosophy of Mind. Cambridge University Press.
233. Searle, J. R. (1980). Minds, brains, and programs. Behavioral and Brain Sciences, 3(3), 417-424.
234. Searle, J. R. (2004). Mind: A brief introduction. Oxford University Press.
235. Shields, C. (2016). Aristotle. Routledge.
236. Skinner, B. F. (1953). Science and Human Behavior. Macmillan.
237. Sloman, L. (2000). 'Thinking through Feeling: the Hole of Emotions in Newer Organizing' . Journal of Psychosomatic Research.
238. Smith, J. (2020). Consciousness and Neuroscience: Bridging the Gap. Journal of Consciousness Studies, 27(3), 123-148.
239. Smith, S. M., Beckmann, C. F., & Andersson, J. (2020). Advances in functional and structural MR image analysis and implementation as FSL. *NeuroImage*, 62(2), 782-790.
240. Squire, L. R., & Zola-Morgan, S. (1991). The medial temporal lobe memory system. Science, 253(5026), 1380-1386.
241. Stapp, H. P. (2007). Mindful Universe: Quantum Mechanics and the Participating Observer. Springer.
242. Stoljar, D. (2001). Two conceptions of the physical. Philosophy and Phenomenological Research, 62(2), 253-281.
243. Stoljar, D. (2015). Physicalism. In E.N. Zalta (Ed.), The Stanford Encyclopedia of Philosophy (Spring 2015 Edition).
244. Strawson, G. (2006). Realistic monism: Why physicalism entails panpsychism. In A. Freeman (Ed.), Consciousness and its place in nature. Imprint Academic.
245. Strawson, G. (2006). Consciousness and Its Place in Nature. Imprint Academic.
246. Strawson, G. (2006). Realistic monism: Why physicalism entails panpsychism. Journal of Consciousness Studies, 13(10-11), 3-31.
247. Strawson, G. (2006). Realistic monism: Why physicalism entails panpsychism. Journal of Consciousness Studies, 13(10-11), 3-31.
248. Tegmark, M. (2017). Life 3.0: Being Human in the Age of Artificial Intelligence. Knopf.
249. Tononi, G. (2008). Consciousness as integrated information: a provisional manifesto. Biological Bulletin, 215(3), 216-242.

250. Tononi, G. (2012). Integrated Information Theory of Consciousness: An updated account. Archives Italiennes de Biologie, 150, 290-326.
251. Tononi, G., & Koch, C. (2015). Consciousness: Here, there and everywhere? Philosophical Transactions of the Royal Society B: Biological Sciences, 370(1668), 20140167.
252. Turing, A. M. (1950). Computing machinery and intelligence. Mind, 59(236), 433-460.
253. Velmans, M., & Schneider, S. (Eds.). (2007). *The Blackwell companion to consciousness*. Blackwell Publishing.
254. Vygotsky, L. (1986). Thought and Language. MIT Press.
255. Whorf, B. L. (1956). Language, Thought, and Reality: Selected Writings of Benjamin Lee Whorf. MIT Press.
256. Wundt, W. (1902). Principles of Physiological Psychology. Swan Sonnenschein & Co.